infuse

Herbal teas to cleanse,
nourish and heal

**PAULA GRAINGER
& KAREN SULLIVAN**

hamlyn

Contents

Introduction 6

Blending for Wellbeing 10

CLEANSE & DETOX 20

DIGEST & NOURISH 36

BOOST & REVITALIZE 52

PEACE & CALM 68

FORTIFY & PROTECT 84

BLISS & HAPPINESS 100

BEYOND TEA 118

Herb-pedia 132

Resources 140

Index 142

Acknowledgements 144

Introduction

Herbs have been used for their medicinal qualities for millennia to treat a broad range of physical and emotional health conditions, and to support health and wellbeing on all levels. Over the years, a wealth of studies has shown how effective they can be. St John's wort has been used successfully in the treatment of depression, echinacea has been proven to treat and prevent flu and colds, ginger is effective for nausea, indigestion and motion sickness, and peppermint has been clinically proven to ease the symptoms of Irritable Bowel Syndrome (IBS). Many plants have been synthesized to create modern medicines such as morphine (from poppies), digoxin (from foxglove; used to treat heart disease) and aspirin (from white willow bark).

Not only do herbs have numerous and powerful healing benefits, they are also rich in nutrients that can keep illness at bay and promote glowing good health. Many are prescribed for specific effects on the body, or as support for the natural healing process, and work by strengthening organs and body systems, such as the digestive or immune systems. As the body is strengthened by herbs, so is its ability to fight disease.

While there are numerous ways to prepare and use herbs, herbal teas are quick and easy to make, and drinking them is a soothing, restorative way of experiencing their healing powers. Best of all, you can use fresh herbs and flowers from your garden, spices from your store cupboard, and take advantage of the thousands of therapeutic herbs now available online to create delicious herbal brews at minimal cost.

Served hot, chilled or even frozen into ice cubes or ice lollies (perfect for younger members of the family), herbal teas can be sipped throughout the day. And they can be prepared especially to address specific symptoms or shore up a system that may be struggling in times of stress, for example, or after a period of illness, lack of sleep or because of poor eating habits. Their restorative powers cannot be underestimated. Some work quickly and effectively to tackle common symptoms, such as coughs, sore throats, insomnia, tummy upsets and cystitis, while others work over time to address deeper-rooted problems, such as blood sugar and hormonal imbalances, arthritis and other inflammatory diseases, chronic pain and skin conditions such as eczema and psoriasis.

Perhaps most importantly, many herbs can also have a dramatic effect on emotional health, easing anxiety, depression, sleep problems, mood swings, symptoms of stress and even helping with overall brain function, in the case of dementia, poor concentration, memory problems and more!

This beautiful book is full of delicious recipes designed to prevent and treat dozens of common health problems using a cornucopia of herbs to make blends that will nourish, support and treat with every sip.

In the Cleanse & Detox chapter (see page 20) you will find teas to cleanse your body of toxins that may be affecting your overall health, aiding the digestive system, your liver, kidneys and skin. Some digestive problems affect the body's absorption of nutrients from food, resulting in distressing symptoms that affect your quality of life. In the Digest & Nourish chapter (see page 36), you will find a selection of nourishing, healing teas with which you will see your symptoms relieved and your energy levels soar.

Our busy lifestyles put pressure on every system in our bodies, and from time to time it is essential to nudge those systems into action to ensure we look and feel our best. Whether you need a kick-start in the morning to raise energy levels, or a selection of herbs designed to help you sharpen your memory, ease chronic pain or cope with life's challenges, you will find everything you need in the Boost & Revitalize chapter (see page 52) to help you get back on track.

Equally important are the teas in the Peace & Calm chapter (see page 68). These encourage profound relaxation and a sense of peace, to help you become more resilient in periods of stress or illness, and to address depression, hormonal highs and lows, headaches and poor-quality sleep. When you are rested and feeling positive and balanced, you will feel more able to face the challenges ahead.

Fortify & Protect (see page 84) is bursting with healing, restorative teas that not only work to boost your immune system and any other systems affected by ill health, but also ease symptoms and encourage the body's natural healing energies. Essential in the winter months, or when you have burned the candle at both ends, these soothing, nourishing teas will relax, invigorate or restore – whatever your body needs to shore up its defences to keep you operating at top gear.

The fragrant, uplifting teas in the chapter Bliss & Happiness (see page 100) will help to set you on a course to top health on every level. If your relationship – and your sex life – needs a boost, your 'vital force' needs strengthening, or you simply need an emotional pick-me-up to encourage calm, restful sleep, and feelings of contentment and even joy as you go about your day, there is something here for you.

Finally, we take you Beyond Tea (see page 116), to some nutritious milks, honeys and fresh, fragrant goodies to enhance the health benefits of the teas in this book, or that can work on their own to support health and wellbeing.

If you're pregnant, breastfeeding or taking medication, look out for the symbols in the key below on the tea recipes and steer clear of those particular teas for the time being.

At the end of this book is a useful compendium of herbs that outlines their key healing benefits and any contraindications they may have (see the Herb-pedia, pages 132–9). Use this to create your own blends, based on your own individual symptoms and needs, or to learn more about the wonderful world of herbs.

All that remains now is to sit back, sip and watch your health and wellbeing soar. Happy drinking!

KEY TO TEAS

♥ avoid during pregnancy

◐ avoid when breastfeeding

◉ avoid when taking medication

Blending for Wellbeing

There are different ways in which you can create nourishing, supportive and actively healing teas to improve your health and wellbeing. Some are dependent upon the types of herbs you are using; for example, woodier herbs need to be chopped and boiled or 'decocted', while fresh herbs and flowers simply need a gentle infusion in not-quite boiling water to release their healing powers. In this section, you will find some useful tips to help you get the most from your herbs and the teas you will create with them.

Equipment

You don't need a lot of equipment to prepare delicious herbal infusions, and you probably already own some of the items listed below. But the right equipment can help you get the best from your herbs, so it is worth considering investing in a few special items.

To make the teas in this book, you will need the following equipment:

- **LARGE TEAPOT** – a glass one shows off the herbs
- **SMALL TEAPOT** – those with built-in infusers work really well for herb teas, as they are quick and easy to clean
- **TEA STRAINER**
- **MEDIUM-SIZED STRAINER**
- **PESTLE AND MORTAR** – the bigger/heavier, the better
- **SPICE OR COFFEE GRINDER** – if using a coffee grinder, reserve it for herbs to avoid everything tasting of coffee. Clean your grinder after use by running through a couple of tablespoons of plain dry rice
- **1 LITRE MEASURING JUG**, preferably glass
- **LARGE GLASS OR CHINA SERVING JUG** for iced teas
- **SET OF MEASURING SPOONS**
- **TEA BALL OR TEA INFUSER** – get a large one with lots of space to allow the herbs to move around as they infuse
- **ELECTRIC OR STOVE-TOP KETTLE**

- **SMALL SAUCEPAN**
- **WATER FILTER**
- **GLASS STORAGE JARS OR TINS** to keep your dried herbs in tip-top condition
- **LABELS**, so you remember which herb is in which jar.

Buying dried herbs

All the dried herbs in this book should be obtainable from herbal suppliers. You will find a list of online suppliers who sell herbs in small quantities in the resources section (see page 140), but it is also worth checking out your local health food shop or a specialist herb shop if you have one nearby, as many have a good selection of dried herbs, and are staffed by people who are knowledgeable and enthusiastic about all things herbal.

While dried herbs have good keeping properties, they do degrade over time, especially if they are stored in warm conditions or under bright light, which can cause them to lose some of their medicinal properties as well as flavour. When you are buying dried herbs, use your senses to check for freshness. Flowers and leaves should retain some colour; seeds, roots and bark should be firm to the touch.

Your sense of smell can be a great guide – the herbs should smell fresh and bright. If they smell musty or 'off', find another supplier.

Most herbs are sold in paper or plastic bags, so it is a good idea to transfer them into containers such as jars or tins with a tight-fitting lid once you bring them home. A shelf full of dried herbs displayed in clear glass jars looks beautiful, but unless you are using them quickly, herbs stored in clear glass can be damaged by light, so keep them in a cupboard or use dark-coloured glass jars or tins, and keep them away from direct heat. Always label your herb containers – you may think you will remember what's what, but even the most experienced herbalists can get confused.

Basic herb kit

There are so many herbs you can choose for their flavour and medicinal benefits, but with such an abundance of herbs available, starting out can be daunting. The selection of herbs given below will make up a useful and effective basic herbal apothecary. Don't worry if you are missing a particular ingredient in a recipe, you can simply leave it out or use a little more of some of the others.

Our basic herb kit contains:

- CALENDULA
- CHAMOMILE
- CINNAMON STICKS
- ECHINACEA
- ELDERBERRIES
- LEMON BALM
- LINDEN FLOWER
- LIQUORICE (CHOPPED)
- MEADOWSWEET
- PEPPERMINT
- SAGE
- SKULLCAP

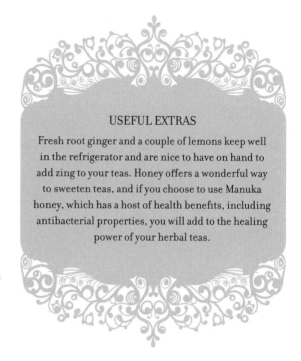

USEFUL EXTRAS

Fresh root ginger and a couple of lemons keep well in the refrigerator and are nice to have on hand to add zing to your teas. Honey offers a wonderful way to sweeten teas, and if you choose to use Manuka honey, which has a host of health benefits, including antibacterial properties, you will add to the healing power of your herbal teas.

Obtaining fresh herbs

It is lovely to include fresh herbs in your infusions. Their taste and aroma add brightness and they make beautiful garnishes. Even if you don't have a garden, growing a few fresh herbs doesn't take up a lot of space – a window box or sunny windowsill is enough, provided you feed and water the plants well. Lemon balm, mint, sage and thyme are easy herbs to grow and will all reward you for regular snipping by putting on new, lush growth to provide a constant supply of fresh leaves.

WILDCRAFTING

The practice of collecting herbs from wild or public spaces is called 'wildcrafting'. There are several things to consider before you set out with your basket and snippers, and these are listed on page 15. But don't let these put you off – herb hunting adds a wonderful dimension to a walk and children will have great fun while fostering a greater connection with nature.

- Correctly identifying the plant is essential! Invest in a good field guide and look online for pictures and descriptions of the plants you hope to pick. It is worth contacting a local herbalist to see whether they offer local herb walks. This is a great way to learn to identify the medicinal plants growing in your neighbourhood from an expert. It is a good idea to take your camera and carefully photograph the herbs you come across for future reference.

- There are usually strict laws about what can be taken from publicly owned land, so familiarize yourself with the rules for the area in which you are planning to pick. It is illegal to collect plants from privately owned land without the owner's permission. Although, if you spot an abundance of dandelions in a neighbour's garden, don't be afraid to knock on the door and politely ask whether you can harvest – you may be doing them a favour!

- Many plants are under threat in the wild and it is important to wildcraft in an ethical and responsible manner. As a general rule, don't take roots or bark, which will damage the plant. Also, limit yourself to picking less than 10 per cent of flowers or leaves from a single area. If you are unsure whether a plant is endangered, research online to check before picking, and never collect any plant that is considered rare.

- To avoid pollutants, pesticides or other nasties, avoid picking from the edges of busy roads, and check online to ensure the area is not polluted by previous industrial use. Also, avoid non-organic farmland, which can look completely natural but may carry the residue of pesticides and fertilizers. Local authorities are a good source of information about which chemicals their gardeners use in parks and recreational areas. Avoid places that are popular with dog walkers when you are collecting low-growing herbs.

HERBS ON HAND

Why not choose a few favourite tea recipes and blend larger quantities so they are always on hand? Simply scale up the recipe by, for example, 10, then store in a labelled jar or tin. Remember to stir the dried herbs before using as the heavier roots and seeds will tend to sink to the bottom.

Drying herbs for tea

LEAVES AND FLOWERS

It is lovely to extend the bounty of your herb harvest beyond the growing season. Drying your own herbs is easy and it is delightful to enjoy the summer aromas and tastes of your garden on a cold winter's day. A row of bunched herbs, hung up to dry, looks attractive, but it is better to suspend them in clean brown paper bags to avoid showering the floor with fragments of dried herb every time you walk past, and to keep them free of dust and protected from insects.

Harvest your herbs on a dry day, as any moisture can cause the herbs to spoil during the drying process. If you have to pick when they are damp, lay them in a single layer on kitchen paper somewhere warm overnight until they are dry. Morning is considered the best time to pick aromatic herbs, before the heat of the day starts to evaporate their essential oils. For flowering herbs such as calendula and chamomile, snip off flowers as they bloom to encourage more blossoms for repeated harvests. With leafy herbs such as lemon balm and mint, the best time to harvest the whole tops is just as the flowers are coming into bloom. Pick leaves at any time. Remove and discard any dead or mildewed leaves.

If you are harvesting whole stems from plants such as lavender, mint, lemon balm or yarrow, simply snip the stem as long as you can and make small 3–4cm-diameter bunches of the stems. Place a spacious paper bag over the head ends, leaving a little stem poking out of the open end of the bag, and tightly secure the bag around the stems with a rubber band. This can then be used to hang the herbs somewhere warm and dry (an airing cupboard is ideal). The rubber band will tighten as the stems shrink with drying, so that the bag doesn't slip off.

If you are picking flowers, small sprigs, leaves or seeds, simply drop them into a paper bag, making sure to leave plenty of space for air. Tie the top of the bag with string or a rubber band and hang it up to dry.

Leaves and flowers are fully dry if they crumble when rubbed between thumb and forefinger. Strip the leaves from long stems and lightly crush any large leaves so you can fit them into your jar. But try to leave the herbs as intact as possible, as the fewer surface areas that are exposed to the air, the fresher they will remain.

DRYING ROOTS

Roots are best harvested in late autumn or winter, when the plant sends its energy down into the root to be stored and they are at their most potent. Arm yourself with a good sharp spade and stout boots, then dig around the plant and remove as much of the root as you can. If you would like to keep some to grow again next year, this is the time to divide the root (you can do this with the spade or an old bread knife) and replant healthy looking pieces of root, which have visible shoots, adding some good-quality compost and feed to the planting hole and watering in well.

Remove as much soil as possible from the roots you will be drying. You can do this by swooshing them several times in a bucket of water, replacing the water until a final swoosh leaves it clean. A hose and stiff brush will remove really stubborn mud, but bear in mind that you will never get them completely clean. Once the roots are cleaned, lay them out on newspaper somewhere warm and dry. When they are dry to the touch, chop them as finely as you can. Most roots become very tough and hard when dried, so it is best to cut them into pieces of a useful size while they are still fresh.

Being thick and woody, roots need a little heat to help them dry fully. If you have a dehydrating machine, simply follow the manufacturer's instructions. Alternatively, set your oven to its lowest setting and lay the roots in a single layer on baking trays, leaving the oven door slightly ajar. Allow them to dry in the oven for 6–8 hours, checking regularly to ensure they are not burning. This is a task for a day at home, as it is not a good idea to leave them unattended. Once the roots are fully dry (they should snap rather than bend), store them in a labelled jar or tin as you would other dried herbs.

Grinding and powdering herbs

Many herbs are available as powders, and these can be very useful for blending into smoothies or honeys. However, the smaller a herb is cut, the greater its exposure to air and the more quickly it degrades. Breaking tough herbs or spices into smaller pieces immediately before use releases their constituents and helps them infuse or decoct more quickly, so it is worth considering investing in a large, heavy pestle and mortar or a spice or coffee grinder. The aim is not to create a powder, but rather to break the herbs up into smaller pieces. If you don't have a pestle and mortar

or grinder, you can improvise – simply put the herbs in a sealable plastic bag and use a rolling pin to crush them into smaller pieces.

Preparing herb teas

There are two main methods of preparing herbal teas. The aim is always to encourage the precious flavours and medicinal benefits of the herb to be extracted into the water and, for the most part, heat is used to encourage this process.

INFUSIONS

Delicate leaves and flowers need just enough heat to release their constituents into the water. This is particularly true for aromatic herbs such as mint, rosemary, chamomile and thyme, which are high in essential oils that evaporate into the air with prolonged heating. The best way to retain the taste, aroma and medicinal benefits of more fragile herbs is by preparing a simple infusion. Pour hot (but not boiling) water over the herbs and allow them to steep for the length of time specified in the recipe you are following.

DECOCTIONS

Roots, bark and some seeds are usually tough, which means they need a longer infusion time and additional heat. The best way to prepare these herbs is by decocting or gently cooking them in water. Place the herbs and water in a small pan and use a medium heat to slowly bring them to boiling point, then cover the pan with a lid, reduce the heat and simmer gently for the length of time specified in the recipe. If the recipe includes lighter, more aromatic herbs, which might be damaged by longer heat exposure, these can be added once the pan is off the heat and allowed to infuse in the hot decoction in the usual way.

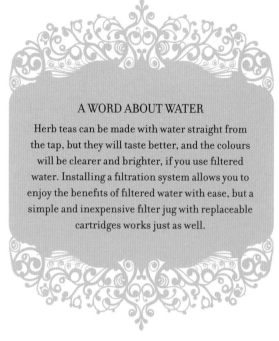

A WORD ABOUT WATER

Herb teas can be made with water straight from the tap, but they will taste better, and the colours will be clearer and brighter, if you use filtered water. Installing a filtration system allows you to enjoy the benefits of filtered water with ease, but a simple and inexpensive filter jug with replaceable cartridges works just as well.

DIY tea blends

Once you have become accustomed to the huge variety of herbs used in this book, and have experienced their medicinal benefits, you may wish to create your own tea blends. There is a very simple template that can help you to create blends that will work to improve your health and wellbeing.

First of all, start with an active ingredient – in other words, a herb that has a direct effect on your body. For example, if you feel a cold brewing, choose something like echinacea or andrographis. Next, choose a herb that will support the part/s of the body affected. In this case, you may choose angelica, which is used traditionally to bring down a fever and treat coughs and colds, or something like couch grass, which can clear mucus, or marshmallow, which soothes the mucus membranes. The final ingredient in your herbal blend will be a herb that compliments the actions of the other herbs. You may choose warming ginger root, cloves or even soothing lavender,

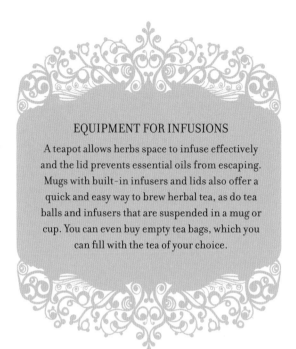

or something like chamomile, which will relax
your body and mind, encouraging restful sleep and
healing. Work on the 3.2.1 principle: three parts
of the active herb/s, two parts of the supportive
herb/s and one part complimentary herbs.

Sweeten or flavour to taste with lemon, honey,
cinnamon, and you will have a personal blend that
is tailored to your individual needs.

Herb teas as gifts

Many of the recipes in this book make great gifts.
Choose an attractive jar and fill it with a blended
herb tea, adding a pretty label listing the ingredients
and method. You can add a tea infuser, mug or
teapot to make it even more special. Children love
to mix tea blends and enjoy decorating the jars and
labels, so get them involved in the gift-making
process. They might also like to use ceramic paints
to decorate a teapot and mug that you can present in
a basket or box alongside your homemade herb tea
blend – a unique and irresistible gift.

A herb is any part of a flower, tree or other
plant – so you may be using the flowers, leaves,
bark, buds, fruits, roots, seeds or even resin from
a plant. The fresher, or more recently picked, the
herb, the stronger its active properties. Dried
herbs are more readily available and are about
one-third as strong as the fresh product.

Herbal teas don't contain traditional teas,
but instead an infusion of healing leaves, berries,
seeds, flowers, bark or roots, whose powers are
extracted with boiling water. The French word
for herbal teas is *tisane*.

There is nothing more soothing than a warm
cup of herbal tea on a cold winter's day, or a fresh,
iced blend with pretty herbal ice cubes to cool you
down when the weather – or your temperament –
is hot. Snuggle up and savour a cup on your own,
or share with friends and family, to raise your
spirits the natural way.

Adding a squeeze of lemon to herbal teas not
only boosts the antioxidant activity of herbs, but
also helps to support liver function, improve
detoxification and support healthy digestion.
Lemon will also reduce any bitterness, particularly
in teas that may have been steeped a little too long.

Almost all herbs work to detoxify the body to some
extent, improving and soothing digestion, and
ridding your organs of toxins to ensure they work at
optimum level. When you are feeling sluggish, tired
and run down, a cup of healing herbal tea may be
all it takes to get you going again.

Chapter One
Cleanse & Detox

One of the most effective ways to encourage optimum health and wellbeing on all levels is to support the organs that work hard to clear out the toxins that can lead to ill health. This fabulous selection of nourishing, tasty teas contains a wealth of herbs that will gently detoxify your body, boost energy levels, balance hormones, encourage clear, healthy skin, aid digestion and stimulate immunity.

Morning Cleanse

Begin each day with this fresh tea for a kick-start to your digestion and lymphatic systems, to help remove waste from your body. It's perfect for when you are feeling listless and lethargic, and is quick and easy to make!

MAKES 1 LARGE MUGFUL

1 sprig of parsley

½ teaspoon dried dandelion leaf or 3–4 fresh leaves

2 lemon slices

1cm piece of fresh root ginger, peeled and roughly chopped

Lightly tear the fresh leaves and fling them into a large mug along with the remaining ingredients. Bring a kettle of filtered water to almost boiling point, then top up the mug with hot water.

TEA TIP

Fresh herbs are lovely in teas and can be very easy to harvest. Dandelion, for example, grows everywhere and, despite its brilliant medicinal quantities, is considered a weed. Why not pluck a few leaves next time you pass a dandelion plant to make this refreshing tea?

Fruity Antioxidant Burst

With vitamin C to detox and a burst of antioxidants from the red and black anthocyanins found in the berries, this flavourful tea boosts the immune system, reduces inflammation and helps to fight free radicals that can lead to degeneration.

MAKES 1 CUP

300ml filtered water

2 teaspoons dried elderberries

1 teaspoon dried bilberries

1 teaspoon dried hibiscus flowers

1 teaspoon dried hawthorn berries

½ teaspoon finely grated orange zest

lemon, for squeezing

honey, to taste

Pour the measured water into a small saucepan and heat it to just below boiling point. Drop in the dried berries and flowers and the orange zest, then reduce the heat to the lowest possible setting and cover the pan with a tight-fitting lid. Simmer gently for 5 minutes until the berries are soft and start to burst.

Strain the mixture into a cup and use the back of a spoon to press as much liquid out of the berries as possible. Add a squeeze of lemon, to taste, for a fresh citrus zing and vitamin C boost, and a little honey, to sweeten.

TEA TIP

Freeze this tea in ice-cube trays and use the ice to flavour water or other cold drinks. Or serve it cooled, over ice, with a sprig of fresh mint.

Bright and Clear Skin ♥

An old adage has it that drinking a cup of cleavers tea every day will create such beauty that no one will be able to resist us! Give it a go — what is there to lose? This refreshing tea features cleansing, nourishing cleavers, complemented by nettle, calendula and burdock, which all help to eliminate toxins for clearer, brighter skin.

MAKES 2 MUGFULS

2 teaspoons dried cleavers

1 teaspoon dried nettle leaf

1 teaspoon dried calendula

½ teaspoon dried chopped burdock root

¼ teaspoon dried chopped orange peel

Put the herbs in a warmed teapot. Bring a kettle of filtered water to just below boiling point and pour 600ml into the teapot, then replace the teapot lid. Leave to infuse for 5–6 minutes, then strain into 2 mugs.

TEA TIP

Harvest your own cleavers, picking the whole stems on a dry day and hanging them, suspended in a paper bag, in a cool dry place until the herb is dry enough to crumble between your fingers. Store the cleavers in a jar to make this wonderful skin-clearing tea all year round.

Skin Fix ♥◉◉

This is great for you if your skin is prone to breakouts. These skin-cleansing herbs work on the liver and lymphatic system to flush away congestion and leave your skin clear and fresh. Add Manuka honey to sweeten and provide antibacterial action.

MAKES 2 CUPS

1 teaspoon dried blue flag

1 teaspoon dried sarsaparilla

½ teaspoon dried calendula

1 teaspoon dried red clover flowers

½ teaspoon dried figwort

Manuka honey, to taste (optional)

Put the dried herbs in a warmed teapot. Bring a kettle of filtered water to just below boiling point, pour 400ml over the herbs and replace the teapot lid. Leave to steep for 10 minutes, then strain into 2 cups and stir in some honey, if using.

TLC (Tea for Liver Care) ♡ ◐

Undoubtedly our body's powerhouse, the liver works hard to take care of us, helping to balance hormones, regulate temperature, aid digestion and cleanse the body. Show your appreciation with cell-restoring milk thistle seed, liver-stimulating dandelion and Oregon grape root, and strengthening schizandra berries. Delicious!

MAKES 2 MUGFULS

2 teaspoons milk thistle seeds

2 teaspoons dried chopped dandelion root

1 teaspoon dried chopped Oregon grape root

2 teaspoons dried schizandra berries

650ml filtered water

2 lemon slices

Using a pestle and mortar or a clean spice grinder, break up the seeds, roots and berries. Empty the herbs into a small saucepan and add the measured water. Bring to the boil, then reduce the heat so that the mixture is just simmering. Let everything gently bubble away for 10 minutes, then remove the pan from the heat and leave to stand for a further 5 minutes. Strain into 2 mugs and garnish each with a lemon slice.

TEA TIP

For a lemony burst, add the lemon slices for the last minute of boiling; lemon is known for its liver-supporting properties.

Bladder Bliss

*Buchu has a glorious blackcurrant aroma and is used in its native South Africa
to support the bladder and kidneys. It is combined here with infection-fighting
bearberry, soothing marshmallow and corn silk as well as diuretic herbs to help
flush an irritated bladder. You can drink the tea just as it is, or mix it half
and half with unsweetened cranberry juice.*

MAKES 1 LITRE

3 teaspoons dried buchu

2 teaspoons dried goldenrod

2 teaspoons dried bearberry leaf

2 teaspoons dried chopped
marshmallow root

1 teaspoon dried couch grass

1 teaspoon dried lemon balm

1 teaspoon dried corn silk

Put the herbs in a large warmed teapot or heatproof glass
jar. Bring a kettle of filtered water to just below boiling
point and pour 1 litre over the herbs. Leave to steep for
5–10 minutes, then strain. Drink some immediately and
allow the remainder to cool, then transfer it to a glass
bottle and store it in the refrigerator for up to 2 days.

TEA TIP

*Drinking plenty of fluids gently flushes the urinary tract when a
bladder infection threatens. Drinking this tea is a tasty and supportive
way in which to do that. This recipe produces a large quantity of tea;
sip it throughout the day for best results.*

Clean Seeds Tea

Aromatic seeds of fennel, fenugreek, celery and aniseed work to balance blood sugar and provide a top-to-toe cleanse. Warming ginger and cinnamon spice up the action with their anti-inflammatory and antibacterial qualities. Recent research suggests that cinnamon can lower blood sugar levels and help to prevent type 2 diabetes.

MAKES 1 MUGFUL

1½ teaspoons fennel seeds

½ teaspoon celery seeds

¼ teaspoon fenugreek seeds

1 teaspoon dried chopped ginger or 1cm piece of fresh root ginger, peeled and chopped

½ teaspoon aniseed

¼ teaspoon ground cinnamon or dried fine chips

lemon slices, to garnish

Put all the ingredients except the garnish into a warmed teapot. Bring a kettle of filtered water to just below boiling point, pour 300ml over the herbs and replace the teapot lid. Leave to steep. Seeds take a little longer to infuse than dried leaves, so it is a good idea to allow the tea to steep for 10–15 minutes. Strain into a mug and serve topped with the lemon slices.

HEALING HERBS

Fennel is a versatile spice with excellent antioxidant properties and loads of vitamins and minerals. It is particularly useful for supporting the digestive system and relieving bloating. Carry a small bag of fennel seeds with you and nibble a few after eating a meal to enhance digestion and freshen your breath.

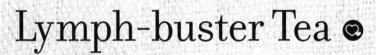

Lymph-buster Tea

The lymphatic system is a crucial part of the immune system. When it becomes overloaded, say, following illness or periods of stress, you can be left feeling sluggish and bloated. This tea can help boost the system. Calendula and cleavers gently stimulate the lymphatic system, while dandelion leaf and horsetail work as diuretics to help clear excess water. Red clover has long been used as a blood cleanser.

MAKES 2 CUPS

2 teaspoons dried dandelion leaf

2 teaspoons dried calendula

1 teaspoon dried cleavers

1 teaspoon dried horsetail

3–4 dried or fresh red clover flowers

honey, to taste (optional)

Put the herbs in a warmed teapot. Bring a kettle of filtered water to just below boiling point and pour 400ml over the leaves, flowers and seeds. Steep for 10 minutes, then strain into 2 cups and enjoy as it is or with a little honey stirred in.

HEALING HERBS

Red clover also helps to improve circulation, providing oxygenated blood to your skin to keep it glowing.

Leafy Green Clean Tea ♥

A bouquet of leaves to spring-clean and nourish your system, this fragrant, delicious combination is warming and satisfying — perfect for a post-winter detox or when you need a boost. Diuretic, nourishing and anti-inflammatory nettle is an important element in this tea and works beautifully with anti-ageing blackberry and raspberry leaves, healing lemon verbena and nutrient-rich oregano, while spearmint not only helps to reduce the effects of stress and tension, but is also a digestive tonic with antifungal properties.

MAKES 2 CUPS

½ teaspoon dried blackberry leaf or 3–4 fresh leaves, torn

½ teaspoon dried nettle leaf

½ teaspoon dried lemon verbena

½ teaspoon dried raspberry leaf

¼ teaspoon dried oregano

¼ teaspoon dried spearmint

¼ teaspoon dried agrimony leaf

2 mint sprigs per serving, to garnish

Mix the leaves well and put them in a warmed teapot. Bring a kettle of filtered water to just below boiling point and pour 400ml over the leaves. Leave to steep for 3–5 minutes, then strain into 2 cups. Serve topped with sprigs of fresh mint.

TEA TIP

Fresh mint leaves make a delightful garnish throughout the year. To enjoy them in wintertime, dig out a small part of your plant in autumn and pot it up in good potting compost. Keep the plant on a sunny windowsill, away from direct heat. You'll be harvesting fresh leaves until spring.

The Morning After the Night Before

Recover your balance and peace of mind after a night of indulgence with milk thistle to support your liver, nettle to cleanse your system, cinnamon to balance blood sugar levels, marshmallow root to soothe troubled digestion, Siberian ginseng to restore energy and lemon balm to lift your battered spirits. You'll feel much better after a cup of this restorative and soothing tea.

MAKES 1 MUGFUL

2 teaspoons milk thistle seeds

1 teaspoon dried nettle leaf

1 teaspoon dried chopped marshmallow root

½ teaspoon dried Siberian ginseng

¼ teaspoon ground cinnamon or ½ cinnamon stick

2 teaspoons dried lemon balm

1 teaspoon honey (optional)

Crush the milk thistle seeds using a pestle and mortar. Put all the herbs, except the lemon balm, in a small pan and add 350ml filtered water. Bring slowly to the boil, then immediately reduce the heat and simmer for 5 minutes. Remove the pan from the heat and add the lemon balm, stirring well. Cover and leave to infuse for 5 minutes. Add the honey, if liked (its complex sugars will help further balance blood sugar levels), strain into a mug and enjoy the sense of peace and wellbeing that ensues.

TEA TIP

Lemon balm has been used for centuries to encourage restful sleep, healthy digestion and a sense of calm. Lemon balm teas are very refreshing, but you can also use this helpful herb in cold drinks. Steep fresh leaves in hot water for 5 minutes, then strain the water and leave it to cool. Pour it into ice-cube trays and freeze. The ice cubes can be used to cool a soothing summer drink.

Chapter Two
Digest & Nourish

When your digestive system is in good shape, your body can absorb maximum nutrition from your diet and also expel waste effectively, but when your system struggles to digest, it can leave you feeling tired and unwell. These delicious, stimulating teas will help to keep your digestive system in tip-top condition, and they can also ease uncomfortable symptoms, such as nausea, constipation, bloating, inflammation and heartburn.

Nourishing Rooibos Chai

Warming, comforting and deliciously spicy, Indian chai has become popular in the West. In this chai recipe, rooibos (also known as redbush) replaces the traditional black tea for a delicious caffeine-free drink that is bursting with antioxidants and aromatics. It helps to improve digestion, so you can get the maximum nutrition from your food.

MAKES 2 MUGFULS

2 teaspoons dried rooibos

1 cinnamon stick, broken

3 black peppercorns

4 dried cloves

1 teaspoon dried chopped ginger or 2cm piece of fresh root ginger, peeled and grated

1 teaspoon coriander seeds

3 cardamom pods, lightly crushed

good grating of nutmeg

650ml filtered water

warmed dairy or nut milk, to taste

honey, to taste (optional)

Place all the herbs and seeds in a pan with the measured water. Bring to just below boiling point, then reduce the heat so that the water is just bubbling. Cover with a tight-fitting lid and leave to gently bubble away for 10 minutes. Turn off the heat and allow the chai to infuse for another 5 minutes, then strain into 2 mugs. Adding just a splash of warmed dairy or nut milk, such as Almond Milk (see page 123), and a little honey allows the spices to really sing, or for a more traditional (and delightfully comforting) brew, add 100ml warmed milk and 1 teaspoon honey.

Move It!

*Most of us suffer from constipation from time to time, with its accompanying
discomfort and bloating. Sip this tea at bedtime and you may wake up to relief.
Rhubarb root and yellow dock gently stimulate movement, while cramp bark,
chamomile and aromatic spices prevent pain.*

MAKES 1 MUGFUL

2 teaspoons dried chopped
rhubarb root

1 teaspoon dried chopped
yellow dock root

1 teaspoon dried chopped cramp bark

¼ teaspoon coriander seeds

¼ teaspoon aniseed

¼ teaspoon dried finely chopped
orange peel

325ml filtered water

1 teaspoon dried chamomile flowers

Place all the ingredients, except the chamomile, in a
small saucepan with the measured water. Slowly bring the
brew to boiling point, then reduce the heat and simmer
for 5 minutes. Remove the pan from the heat and toss in
the chamomile flowers. Cover with a tight-fitting lid and
leave to steep for 5 minutes. Strain well into a large mug.

HEALING HERBS

*If you are prone to constipation, sipping a cup of this delicious
tea once or twice a week can help to keep the problem at bay.*

No More Nausea

Nausea is a symptom rather than a condition in itself, so it is always worth finding out the cause. This tea can help to relieve nausea and is safe and effective for occasional use for travel sickness, early pregnancy and nervous queasiness. Take small, slow sips until the discomfort has eased.

MAKES 1 CUP

1 teaspoon dried black horehound

1cm piece of fresh root ginger, peeled and finely sliced

1 teaspoon dried peppermint or a small handful of fresh leaves

Put the herbs in a warmed teapot. Bring a kettle of filtered water to just below boiling point and pour 250ml into the teapot, then replace the teapot lid. Leave to steep for 5 minutes, then strain into a cup.

TEA TIP

Ensure you do not confuse the ingredient black horehound with the bitter expectorant white horehound, which is used for chesty coughs.

Nervous Tummy Tea

*A stressful situation is made far worse by having to dash to the loo — the result
of your body's natural fight-or-flight stress response. Stay on task with this helpful
tea, which features astringent agrimony and hawthorn, and also antispasmodic
cramp bark. Spearmint, vervain and skullcap will help to calm your nerves.*

MAKES 1 CUP

1 teaspoon dried agrimony leaf

1 teaspoon dried hawthorn
leaves and flowers

1 teaspoon dried chopped cramp bark

1 teaspoon dried skullcap leaf

½ teaspoon dried spearmint

½ teaspoon dried vervain leaf

Put all the herbs in a warmed teapot. Bring a kettle
of filtered water to just below boiling point and pour
250ml into the teapot, then replace the teapot lid. Leave
to steep for 15 minutes. Strain into 1 cup, or allow to cool
and carry in a sports bottle or Thermos flask for a calm
tummy on the go.

TEA TIP

*Use fully boiling water and a longer infusion time for this tea to
release more tannins — the astringent constituents in agrimony
and hawthorn that control a runny tummy.*

Tummy Warmer Tea

Traditional systems of medicine from around the world tend to blame poor digestion on a cold, damp digestive system. This warming blend of herbs and spices will help restore function and improve your body's ability to draw nourishment from the food you eat.

MAKES 2 CUPS

1 teaspoon fennel seeds

1 teaspoon dried chopped angelica root

1 teaspoon dried chamomile flowers

2 cardamom pods

½ teaspoon dill seeds

¼ teaspoon caraway seeds

1cm piece of fresh root ginger, peeled and finely sliced

1 cinnamon stick, halved

1 star anise

Put all the herbs except the star anise into a large warmed teapot. Bring a kettle of filtered water to just below boiling point and pour 450ml into the teapot, then replace the teapot lid. Leave to steep for 15 minutes, then strain. Leave to cool a little, then pour the liquid into 2 warmed cups and drop in the star anise to float prettily on the surface.

HEALING HERBS

Star anise gives foods and drinks a pleasant aniseed flavour, but it has also been used for centuries in herbal medicine, to treat and prevent viruses and act as an antifungal, among other things.

Gut Soother

Tea doesn't have to be hot! The mucilage (a gooey substance produced by many plants) found in the herbs in this recipe can be extracted into water without the need to apply heat, allowing you to make a delicious cold infusion. This tea is an unbeatable remedy for an inflamed gut, Irritable Bowel Syndrome (IBS) or food intolerances.

MAKES 3 SMALL GLASSFULS

1 teaspoon dried chopped marshmallow root

1 teaspoon dried plantain leaf

1 teaspoon liquorice root powder

1 teaspoon slippery elm powder

500ml filtered water

Roughly crush the marshmallow root, plantain leaf and liquorice powder using a pestle and mortar. (A clean spice-grinder works well for this job, too.) Place the crushed herbs with the slippery elm powder into a lidded jar and add the measured water. Shake well and leave overnight in a cool place.

The next morning, strain the mixture into a jug through a fine sieve lined with muslin. Once the liquid has drained through the muslin, squeeze out the muslin to extract as much water from the herbs as possible. Store in a glass bottle in the refrigerator where it will keep for up to 36 hours. Sip a glassful before meals.

Digesti-tea

Meadowsweet is a deliciously fragrant herb and such a good remedy for indigestion that you can use it on its own. However, combined with linden flower, chamomile and a little peppermint to soothe heartburn and acidity, it is even more effective. Drinking this tea is the perfect way to ease indigestion on the spot.

MAKES 2 CUPS

2 teaspoons dried meadowsweet

1 teaspoon dried linden flowers

1 teaspoon dried chamomile blossoms

½ teaspoon dried peppermint

1 mint leaf per serving, to garnish

Put all the herbs in a warmed teapot. Bring a kettle of filtered water to just below boiling point and pour 400ml into the teapot, then replace the teapot lid. Leave to infuse for 10 minutes. Strain into 2 cups and garnish each with a mint leaf.

Bitter and Twisted

*Alcoholic bitters are taken all over the world as pre-dinner aperitifs to stimulate appetite
and increase the flow of digestive juices. This bitters recipe has all the health benefits,
but cuts out the alcohol. Take a small glassful before meals or add a little sparkling water
and lemon juice to make your own delightfully tart and aromatic digestif.*

MAKES 500ML

1 teaspoon dried mugwort

1 teaspoon dried chopped orange
peel or fresh orange zest

½ teaspoon dried chopped
elecampane root

½ teaspoon dried chopped
angelica root

½ teaspoon coriander seeds

½ teaspoon dried chopped
Oregon grape root

¼ teaspoon dried lavender flowers

¼ teaspoon dried rosemary

500ml filtered water

Put the ingredients in a small saucepan. Slowly heat until
just below boiling point, then reduce the heat to the lowest
setting and simmer, covered, for 10 minutes. Remove from
the heat and leave to cool completely. Strain the mixture well,
then transfer to a glass bottle. Store in the refrigerator for
2–3 days.

HEALING HERBS
*Oregon grape root has long been used to stimulate the flow
of bile from the liver, which encourages the digestive process.
Including bitter herbs and salad leaves such as rocket or
chicory in your diet will support good digestion.*

Post-prandial Tea

This tea is mouth-wateringly refreshing and offers the perfect way to finish off a meal, especially if you happen to have overindulged in rich foods. These tummy-soothing herbs will gently reduce bloating to help you feel more comfortable and ready for a good night's sleep. Seek medical advice before taking this tea if you have high blood pressure.

MAKES 2 MUGFULS

2 teaspoons fennel seeds

1 teaspoon dried chopped liquorice root

½ teaspoon dried peppermint

½ teaspoon dried lemon balm

1 cardamom pod, lightly crushed

Put all the herbs in a warmed teapot. Bring a kettle of filtered water to just below boiling point and pour 600ml into the teapot, then replace the teapot lid. Leave to steep for 5 minutes, then strain into 2 mugs.

HEALING HERBS

Cardamom has a whole host of health benefits — it reduces acidity, bloating, constipation and bad breath, and can also help to lower blood pressure.

Gut Reaction

Soreness and inflammation of the digestive system can be caused by a number of things, including a bout of food poisoning or a stomach virus, food intolerance and conditions such as IBS. The presence of large numbers of nerve cells in the digestive system means that anxiety and stress can also cause digestive issues. This effective tea combines four ingredients that have powerful anti-inflammatory properties with herbs that relax the nervous system. This tea is not suitable if you have high blood pressure or an oestrogenic condition.

MAKES 2 MUGFULS

1 teaspoon dried chopped wild yam root

1 teaspoon dried plantain leaf

½ teaspoon dried albizia bark or flowers

650ml filtered water

1 teaspoon dried meadowsweet

½ teaspoon dried chopped liquorice root

½ teaspoon dried lemon balm

½ teaspoon dried tulsi (holy basil)

honey, to taste (optional)

Place the wild yam, plantain and albizia in a pan, pour in the measured water and bring to just below boiling point. Remove the pan from the heat and immediately drop in the remaining herbs. Cover tightly and steep for 10 minutes. Strain into 2 mugs and sweeten with a little honey, if liked.

HEALING HERBS
Tulsi, also known as holy basil, is an extremely versatile and popular herb. One study found that it helps to balance cortisone (the stress hormone) levels in the body and ease headaches. A simple daily cup of tulsi tea may also help balance blood sugar levels.

Chapter Three
Boost & Revitalize

Herbs can provide an extraordinarily powerful boost both to energy levels and low spirits, and help to keep your mind and senses sharp and operating at optimum levels. Whether you are in need of a pick-me-up after a tough day, a helping hand during exams or periods of stress or ill health, or something to bring balance when things go off-kilter, this healing, restorative selection of teas can provide nourishment and healing on many levels, leaving you feeling fresh, invigorated and ready for action.

Dandelion 'Coffee'

*If you rely on coffee to get you going in the mornings, why not try this delicious
caffeine-free alternative that supports your liver and digestive system?
Dandelion and chicory lend a satisfying coffee-like bitterness, which is
rounded out by the sweet spiciness of fennel, cinnamon and liquorice.
Avoid drinking this tea if you have high blood pressure.*

MAKES 2 MUGFULS

2 teaspoons roasted dandelion root

2 teaspoons roasted chicory

½ teaspoon fennel seeds

½ teaspoon dried chopped liquorice root

600ml filtered water

1 cinnamon stick per serving, to garnish

Put the dandelion, chicory, fennel seeds and liquorice
in a small pan. Add the measured water and gently bring
to simmering point. Simmer for 10 minutes, then strain
into 2 mugs, adding a cinnamon stick to each for stirring.

TEA TIP

*You can buy ready-roasted dandelion root and chicory, but not all herb suppliers
stock them. To roast your own, purchase the roots ready-chopped and dried and lay
them in a single layer on an oven tray. Roast in a preheated oven at 150°C (300°F),
Gas Mark 2 for 30–40 minutes, just until they have turned a rich dark brown.
Keep checking to ensure you do not allow them to become scorched. Leave to
cool, then store in airtight glass or metal containers.*

Memory Boost Tea

If 'senior moments' have you hunting for your keys or standing in the kitchen trying to remember just what you came in for, try a regular cup of this delicious blend of memory-boosters. Many of the ingredients have long-term benefits that could help to prevent dementia. Drink a cup, hot or cold, daily. Note that gingko should be taken only under medical supervision if you are on blood-thinning medication.

MAKES 2 MUGFULS

1 teaspoon dried gotu kola

1 teaspoon dried lemon balm

1 teaspoon dried tulsi (holy basil)

1 teaspoon dried gingko leaf

½ teaspoon dried rosemary or 1 small sprig of fresh rosemary

¼ teaspoon dried bacopa leaf

1cm piece of fresh root ginger, finely sliced

Put the herbs in a warmed teapot and mix well to ensure the tea is blended. Bring a kettle of filtered water to just below boiling point and pour 600ml into the teapot, then replace the teapot lid. Leave to infuse for 5 minutes, then strain into 2 mugs.

TEA TIP

Bacopa, also known as brahmi, is a popular herb used in Ayurvedic (traditional Indian) medicine. Research suggests that it can help to encourage the regeneration of brain cells and provide protection against the degeneration associated with Alzheimer's disease.

Post-exercise Pick-me-up

Enjoy this revitalizing tea after working out to restore energy, soothe tired muscles and reduce inflammation. Turmeric and a little honey help to balance your blood sugar, while damiana induces an instant sense of wellbeing. Taken in large quantities, liquorice may exacerbate high blood pressure, so is best avoided if this applies to you. Note also that meadowsweet is not suitable for people who are allergic to aspirin.

MAKES 1 CUP

1 teaspoon dried meadowsweet

1 teaspoon dried chopped wild yam root

1 teaspoon dried damiana leaf

½ teaspoon dried chopped liquorice root

⅛ teaspoon ground turmeric

200ml filtered water

Manuka honey, to taste (optional)

Put all the herbs into a small pan and add the measured water. Slowly bring to the boil, then reduce the heat to its lowest setting, cover the pan with a lid and simmer for 5 minutes. Remove the pan from the heat and strain the tea into a cup. Add a little honey, if liked.

HEALING HERBS
Manuka honey has antiseptic and antibiotic properties, and is a natural anti-inflammatory and pain reliever. To be effective, it needs a minimum rating of 10 UMF (Unique Manuka Factor).

Liq-a-mint

This delicious, refreshing infusion is the perfect tea to enjoy at any time of day. Mint is cooling and energizing, while liquorice boosts energy levels and acts as a tonic. Avoid drinking this tea if you have high blood pressure.

MAKES 1 CUP

1 teaspoon peppermint (fresh or dried)

1 teaspoon spearmint (fresh or dried)

½ teaspoon dried chopped liquorice root

mint leaf, to garnish

Bring a kettle of filtered water to just below boiling point. Put the herbs in a large tea infuser and place this in a cup. Pour over approximately 200ml hot water. Steep for 5 minutes and enjoy garnished with a fresh mint leaf.

TEA TIP
This tea is good chilled, and as both liquorice and mint are great digestive herbs, it will help with gassiness and bloating.

Get Up and Go Tea ♥◌

Delightfully refreshing, this morning tea can also be enjoyed whenever you need an energy boost. Damiana, sarsaparilla and Siberian ginseng sharpen the mind, while peppermint and lemon grass deliver a zingy wake-up call to the senses.

MAKES 1 LARGE MUGFUL

1 teaspoon dried damiana leaf

1 teaspoon dried sarsaparilla

1 teaspoon dried Siberian ginseng

1 teaspoon dried lemon grass or 2cm fresh lemon grass, crushed

½ teaspoon dried peppermint

Bring a kettle of filtered water to just below boiling point. Put all the herbs in a spacious tea infuser and drop it into a large mug. Pour over 300ml hot water. Allow to infuse for 10 minutes, occasionally swirling the infuser in the water. Strain and drink hot or cold.

TEA TIP

Try this tea when you are jetlagged. Russian cosmonauts on the Soviet space programme used Siberian ginseng to alleviate fatigue and increase stamina!

Study-aid Tea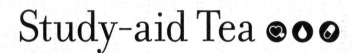

This brain-boosting blend is the one to tuck into your backpack before you head off to university. With gingko and rosemary for memory, damiana and ginger to maximize concentration, and skullcap to help you feel calm, yet alert, it will help to keep the brain firing on all cylinders! This tea is best avoided if you have high blood pressure or take blood-thinning medication.

MAKES 1 MUGFUL

1 teaspoon dried damiana leaf

1 teaspoon dried gingko leaf

½ teaspoon dried skullcap leaf

½ teaspoon dried rosemary

¼ teaspoon dried ginger or 1cm piece of fresh root ginger, chopped

Put the herbs in a warmed teapot. Bring a kettle of freshly filtered water to just below boiling point and pour 300ml into the teapot, then replace the teapot lid. Leave to steep for 5–10 minutes, then strain into a mug and drink hot or cold.

TEA TIP

Around exam time, drink this tea when you are revising. Then, if allowed, take a bottle full of the cold tea into the exam with you. The smell and taste will put you into the frame of mind you were in when revising and help you recall what you've learned more easily.

Cool It! ♥ ◐

*When the barometer is rising and you need something light and refreshing
to cool you down, make this fresh-tasting chilled tea. All these herbs, apart
from the elderflowers, can be easily grown in your garden or on a windowsill
and snipped for use as required for a really delicious brew.*

MAKES 2 TALL GLASSFULS

2 teaspoons chopped fresh spearmint

2 teaspoons dried or fresh elderflowers

1 teaspoon chopped fresh sage

1 teaspoon chopped dried violet leaf

pinch of fresh or dried lavender flowers

ice, to serve

To garnish

1 slice of lemon per serving

1 sprig of fresh lavender per serving

Put the herbs in a warmed teapot. Bring a kettle of filtered water to just below boiling point and pour 600ml into the teapot, then replace the teapot lid. Leave to steep for 20 minutes, then strain the tea into a jug and allow it to cool completely. Refrigerate the tea until you are ready to drink it and serve it in 2 tall glasses, over ice, with a slice of lemon and a lavender sprig in each glass.

TEA TIP

*Flavours are suppressed when you serve an infusion cold, so this
recipe uses more herbs and allows the tea to steep a little longer than
usual to retain their fresh taste. If you like the idea of serving any of
your brews cold, bear this in mind and experiment with increasing
the quantities of herbs and/or steeping time.*

I'm a Mum Tea

*Becoming a mother is exciting, life-changing — and not just a little
exhausting! This tea supports you and your baby, with fennel and fenugreek
to increase milk production, nettle for a nourishing boost of essential minerals,
raspberry leaf to help restrengthen your womb and peppermint for digestive
comfort. Fennel has been shown to travel through breast milk, easing colic and
wind in your baby. If you can, take a few minutes while the baby sleeps to
put your feet up and relax while sipping your tea.*

MAKES 1 MUGFUL

2 teaspoons fennel seeds

1 teaspoon fenugreek seeds

1 teaspoon dried raspberry leaf

1 teaspoon dried nettle leaf

½ teaspoon dried peppermint

Put the herbs in a warmed teapot. Bring a kettle of filtered
water to just below boiling point and pour 300ml into the
teapot, then replace the teapot lid. Leave to steep for
5–10 minutes, then strain into a mug.

TEA TIP

*It is a busy time for a mum when her baby is a newborn, so why not
scale up the quantities to prepare a jar of this blend before your baby
arrives, so it is ready when you need it? This tea makes a delightful
and useful baby shower gift, presented in a beautifully decorated jar.
Add a cute label with the names of the herbs, and instructions
to use 1–2 teaspoons per cup of boiling water.*

Achy Joint Tea ♥💧

This tea contains a blend of powerful anti-inflammatory herbs to help ease the discomfort of swollen, achy joints. Rosehips and meadowsweet round out the strong flavours of turmeric and willow bark. Avoid drinking this tea if you are allergic to aspirin.

MAKES 1 MUGFUL

1 teaspoon dried rosehips

1 teaspoon dried meadowsweet

1 teaspoon dried willow bark

1 teaspoon dried Devil's Claw

¼ teaspoon ground turmeric

¼ teaspoon celery seeds

300ml filtered water

honey, to taste (optional)

Put all the herbs into a small saucepan with the measured water. Heat the tea to just below boiling point, then reduce the heat and simmer for 5 minutes. Remove the pan from the heat and allow to cool a little, then strain well into a mug. Stir in a little honey while the tea is hot to add sweetness, if desired.

Blood Sugar Balancer

The mid-afternoon energy slump is a common experience that is caused by a blood sugar surge after lunch. Blood sugar levels subsequently plummet, leading to irritability, poor concentration and fatigue. A balanced diet will help, but if you can't resist that slice of cake or sugary muffin, a cup of this tea will help to rebalance your blood sugar levels at once. Drink 1–2 cups, ideally with a small high-protein snack, such as nuts or hummus. If you are taking medication for diabetes, consult a herbalist or health professional before taking this tea.

MAKES 1 CUP

1 teaspoon dried Siberian ginseng

1 cinnamon stick, broken into 2–3 pieces

1 teaspoon dried goats' rue

1 teaspoon dried tulsi (holy basil)

Use a pestle and mortar to break up the Siberian ginseng and cinnamon, then combine them with the other herbs and place them all in a teapot. Bring a kettle of filtered water to just below boiling point and pour 200ml hot water into a warmed teapot, then replace the teapot lid. Allow the tea to infuse for 10 minutes, then strain into a cup.

HEALING HERBS

Goats' rue is often used alongside traditional medication for the treatment of type 2 diabetes.

Chapter Four
Peace & Calm

It is often difficult to find the time and space to relax, unwind and experience pure calm and peace of mind, body and spirit. Supportive, strengthening and serenity-inducing teas can help restore much-needed balance in your life by encouraging deep relaxation and restorative sleep, and bringing relief from pain, emotional turmoil, anxiety and hormonal highs and lows. These are the teas that will keep you going, nurture your spirit and provide profound healing and that all-important feeling of calm.

Laid-back Lemon

A delightfully fresh-tasting tea with a citrus zing to calm the senses, this drink is lovely served either warm or icy cool. Each of the fragrant herbs in this recipe have calming qualities. Linden flowers, in particular, have been shown in a number of studies to reduce anxiety and promote relaxation.

MAKES 2 CUPS

1 teaspoon dried lemon verbena
1 teaspoon dried linden flowers
1 teaspoon dried lemon balm
1 teaspoon dried skullcap leaf
½ teaspoon dried lemon grass
juice of ½ lemon
fresh lemon balm leaf per serving, to garnish

Put the herbs in a warmed teapot. Bring a kettle of freshly filtered water to just below boiling point and pour 400ml into the teapot, then replace the teapot lid. Leave to steep for 10 minutes, then stir in the lemon juice and strain into 2 cups. Serve each cup garnished with a lemon balm leaf.

TEA TIP

When you are buying skullcap, choose the laterifolia variety. Baical skullcap is a close relative, but does not have the same calming properties.

Sweet Sleep Tea

*Like a lullaby in a cup, this sweet blend of sleep-inducing herbs
will relax your mind and body to help prepare you for a wonderful,
restorative night's sleep. Drink a cup an hour before bedtime so the
herbs can start to work their magic before your head hits the pillow.
Omit the hops if you have depression or an oestrogenic condition.*

MAKES 1 LARGE MUGFUL

1 teaspoon dried chamomile flowers
1 teaspoon dried linden flowers
½ teaspoon dried catmint leaf
½ teaspoon dried passionflower
¼ teaspoon dried hop flowers
1 twist of orange zest
pinch of dried lavender flowers

Bring a kettle of filtered water to just below boiling point.
Stuff a spacious tea ball or infuser with the herbs and
place it in a large mug. Pour over enough nearly boiling
filtered water to fill the mug and allow to steep for
5 minutes, then remove the infuser.

TEA TIP

*Because this is a lovely tea to drink each night, it makes sense
to scale up the quantities and keep a stock of the blend in an
airtight jar. Use 3 teaspoons of the mix to quickly and easily
make up a bedtime pot.*

Dream Tea ♥

Many people believe that our dreams carry messages from our subconscious and like to record their dreams in order to gain greater insight into their lives. Mugwort has long been associated with lucid dreaming and many people report that their dreams are more intense and memorable when they take it. Mugwort is bitter, so here it is blended with sweeter-tasting herbs that calm and open the mind. Drink the tea before bedtime and be sure to have your dream diary and a pen on your bedside table!

MAKES 1 CUP

1 teaspoon dried or fresh linden flowers

1 teaspoon dried red clover flowers

½ teaspoon dried California poppy

½ teaspoon dried mugwort

½ teaspoon aniseed

½ teaspoon dried or fresh jasmine flowers

pinch of lavender flowers

wildflower honey, to taste (optional)

Bring a kettle of filtered water to just below boiling point. Put the herbs in a tea infuser and place it in a cup. Pour over enough nearly boiling filtered water to fill the cup and allow to infuse for 5–10 minutes. Add wildflower honey, to taste, if liked.

HEALING HERBS

An old wives' tale tells us that a another way to use mugwort to induce lucid dreaming is to place a fresh leaf under your pillow before going to sleep.

Bon Courage!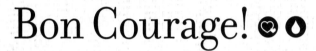

This lovely tea will help to strengthen your resolve and give you a little extra courage when you are facing challenging situations. Before battle, it is said that Roman soldiers recited 'I, borage, always bring courage' and medieval knights went to war with beautiful blue borage flowers embroidered on their clothes. Mugwort is associated with Artemis, the courageous Greek goddess. Lady's mantle is said to protect and lemon balm and skullcap act to dispel anxiety and fear.

MAKES 1 MUGFUL

1 teaspoon dried skullcap leaf

1 teaspoon dried lemon balm

½ teaspoon dried borage (flowers if available, but the leaves work well, too)

½ teaspoon dried lady's mantle

¼ teaspoon dried mugwort

Put the herbs in a small warmed teapot. Bring a kettle of filtered water to just below boiling point and pour 300ml into the teapot, then replace the teapot lid. Leave to steep for 10 minutes, then strain into a mug.

TEA TIP

Conquer your fears in specific situations by carrying a little bottle of this cooled tea to sip on the move. If you double the herb quantities to make a more concentrated tea, it will be effective with smaller sips.

PM Tea ♥

Get swift relief from irritability, bloating and other premenstrual symptoms with this restorative blend. Lemon balm lifts the spirits, dandelion leaf reduces water retention, lady's mantle soothes mind and body, and nettle provides a boost of essential minerals. Drink 1–2 cups as soon as you notice premenstrual symptoms and continue to use this tea until the symptoms recede, drinking up to four cups per day.

MAKES 500ML

1 teaspoon dried lemon balm
1 teaspoon dried dandelion leaf
1 teaspoon dried lady's mantle
1 teaspoon dried nettle leaf

Put the herbs in a warmed teapot. Bring a kettle of filtered water to just below boiling point and pour 500ml into the teapot, then replace the teapot lid. Leave to steep for 10 minutes, then strain.

Monthly Magic ♥ ◊

If you're troubled by menstrual cramps, this tea will help to relieve the discomfort. Antispasmodic cramp bark and Jamaican dogwood relax the uterine muscle, while lady's mantle restores balance. A touch of ginger speeds up the action for fast relief.

MAKES 500ML

3 teaspoons dried chopped cramp bark
1 teaspoon dried lady's mantle
1 teaspoon dried Jamaican dogwood
5mm piece of fresh root ginger, peeled and finely sliced
500ml filtered water
Manuka honey, to taste (optional)

Place all the herbs in a small pan with the measured water. Bring slowly to the boil, then cover the pan with a tight-fitting lid, reduce the heat and simmer for 10 minutes. Turn off the heat and allow the brew to sit for 3–5 minutes, then strain and drink a small glassful every few hours (cold or reheated, according to your preference), sweetened with a little honey, if liked.

TEA TIP
This tea is even more effective if you take it before the menstrual cramps begin. If you have a regular cycle and usually experience pain, start drinking the tea the day before you expect your period and drink 2–3 cups per day for 3–5 days.

Sense of Calm

*Find an oasis of calm in the day with this exquisitely soothing tea.
With oat, passionflower and skullcap to relax and quieten a busy mind,
and rose, tulsi and lemon balm to lighten the spirits, you'll experience
pure relaxation that is hard to find in a busy lifestyle.*

MAKES 1 MUGFUL

1 teaspoon dried oat seed

1 teaspoon dried passionflower

1 teaspoon dried lemon balm

½ teaspoon dried tulsi (holy basil)

½ teaspoon dried skullcap leaf

¼ teaspoon crushed dried rose petals
or 3–4 fresh red or pink petals

Using a pestle and mortar, gently crush the oat seed, then transfer to a warmed teapot and add the remaining herbs. Bring a kettle of filtered water to just below boiling point and pour 300ml into the teapot, then replace the teapot lid. Leave to infuse for 3–5 minutes, then strain into a mug.

HEALING HERBS

*Oat seed is a wonderful herb to use to prevent and treat
symptoms of stress. It soothes the nervous system, improves
brain function and even boosts immunity.*

All in the Mind

*With calming, fragrant lavender, circulation-enhancing rosemary
and fragrant, mood-lifting lemon balm, this is the ideal tea for easing
headaches and symptoms of stress, and putting you in the perfect frame
of mind for complete relaxation. It is also delicious served cold, with
a sprig of fresh lemon balm to garnish.*

MAKES 1 CUP

1 teaspoon fresh rosemary
1 teaspoon dried lemon balm
¼ teaspoon lavender flowers
Manuka honey, to taste (optional)

Put the herbs in a large warmed teapot. Bring a kettle
of filtered water to just below boiling point and pour
200ml into the teapot. Leave to steep for 3–5 minutes,
swirling the herbs in the teapot from time to time.
Strain into a cup and stir in a little honey, if desired.

Stress Headache Tea

*This tea is perfect at the end of one of those days when you haven't had time to catch
a breath and your head is pounding with stress. Chamomile releases tension in your neck
and shoulders, while traditional headache remedies wood betony, feverfew and rosemary
clear your head and ease discomfort. Brew a pot, stretch out, sip two or three cupfuls and
let the herbs gently melt away the pain to restore balance and peace.*

MAKES 1 MUGFUL

2 teaspoons dried chamomile flowers
2 teaspoons dried wood betony
½ teaspoon dried spearmint
¼ teaspoon dried rosemary
¼ teaspoon dried feverfew

Put all the herbs in a small warmed teapot. Bring a
kettle of filtered water to just below boiling point and
pour 300ml into the teapot, then replace the teapot lid.
Leave to steep for 10 minutes, then strain into a mug.

HEALING HERBS
*Feverfew is traditionally used for the treatment of migraines, and
taking a little every day in tea can help to prevent them entirely!*

Time of Your Life Tea ❤ ◐ ◑

This wonderful hormone-settling blend can be used daily to ease the mid-life transition. Chaste tree berries have long been prized for their hormone-balancing action, while shatavari is the classic women's herb in Ayurvedic medicine. Sage and black cohosh help keep you cool and collected, and St John's wort and rose are ideal for the treatment of mood swings. Drink 1–2 cups per day from when you start to experience menopausal symptoms. Avoid drinking this tea if you are taking antidepressant medication.

MAKES 2 CUPS

1 teaspoon dried chaste tree berries

2 teaspoons dried chopped shatavari root

1 teaspoon dried black cohosh

400ml filtered water

2 teaspoons dried sage

½ teaspoon dried St John's wort

few fresh rose petals or ¼ teaspoon crumbled dried petals

Lightly crush the chaste tree berries, shatavari and black cohosh using a pestle and mortar. Transfer the mixture to a saucepan and add the measured water. Heat just to the point where bubbles start appearing on the surface, then simmer very gently for 5 minutes. Remove the pan from the heat and immediately add the sage, St John's wort and rose petals. Cover the pan and leave to infuse for 5 minutes, then strain into 2 cups.

TEA TIP

If hot drinks make hot flushes or night sweats worse, this tea works well cooled and served over ice. Add some fresh berries for colour and extra nutrients.

Is it Warm in Here? ♥ ◑ ●

Feeling a little hot and bothered? This tea is best drunk cold to help manage mid-life hot flushes day and night. Sage is cooling and drying, while motherwort helps with the palpitations that can accompany an episode. Drink a cool cupful at night-time and any time you need refreshing. It's a good idea to carry the cooled tea around in a bottle to cool you down whenever hot flushes strike.

MAKES 1 MUGFUL

2 teaspoons dried sage
2 teaspoons dried red clover
1 teaspoon dried motherwort
1 teaspoon dried lemon verbena
honey, to taste (optional)

Put all the herbs into a large warmed teapot. Bring a kettle of filtered water to just below boiling point and pour 300ml into the teapot, then replace the teapot lid. Leave to steep for 10 minutes (although longer is fine), then strain and add honey to taste. Leave to cool, then keep refrigerated for up to 2 days.

Chapter Five

Fortify & Protect

With nourishing herbs to support the immune system and the adrenal glands, these soothing, delicious teas will not only help to keep ill health at bay, they will also help to keep you strong and healthy, particularly throughout the cold and flu season and in times of stress. If illness does strike, choose from a selection of restorative, healing teas to ease symptoms and get you back on top form. Many of the herbs used for the teas in this chapter are adaptogenic (see page 93), which means they work to uplift or relax, depending upon what your body needs.

Immuni-tea

Working a cup of this tasty tea into your routine offers a simple and enjoyable way to boost the immune system on a daily basis. This blend combines antioxidant-rich elderberry and thyme, astragalus, which encourages resistance to illness, liquorice, which boosts the part of the immune system that fights viruses, and fabulous lemon balm, with its antiviral action. Avoid drinking this tea if you have high blood pressure, since liquorice may exacerbate the condition.

MAKES 1 MUGFUL

2 teaspoons dried elderberries

2 teaspoons dried chopped astragalus root

½ teaspoon dried chopped liquorice root

350ml filtered water

1 teaspoon dried or fresh lemon balm
(fresh leaves have greater antiviral action)

½ teaspoon dried thyme or the leaves
from 2 small sprigs of fresh thyme

honey, to taste (optional)

Put the elderberries, astragalus and liquorice in a small pan with the measured water. Slowly bring to almost boiling point, then reduce the heat and simmer for 3–5 minutes. Remove the pan from the heat and immediately add the lemon balm and thyme. Cover the pan with a lid and leave the tea to infuse for 5 minutes. Strain into a mug and sweeten with a little honey, if desired.

HEALING HERBS
Echinacea is the best-known immune-boosting herb, but it is not included here because many herbalists find it is most effective when used directly before or during a virus.

Commuter Protection ♥○

Packed with vitamin C, antiviral elderberry and bug-fighting cinnamon, echinacea and thyme, this tea is fabulously warming on a cold winter's day and will help to protect you against winter viruses. You can add honey, but the berries and cinnamon lend their own sweetness.

MAKES 1 LARGE MUGFUL

1 teaspoon dried rosehips

½ teaspoon dried elderberries

½ teaspoon dried chopped
echinacea root

¼ teaspoon dried cinnamon
(chopped bark is best, rather than
ground, or use ⅛ cinnamon stick)

¼ teaspoon dried sage or a couple
of fresh leaves

Combine the herbs and pop them into a tea infuser. Put this in a large mug. Bring a kettle of water to just below boiling point and pour the water over the infuser in the mug, swirling the infuser as you pour. Allow the tea to steep for at least 10 minutes so the berries soften and release their goodness, then remove the infuser.

TEA TIP

Carry a Thermos flask full of this piping hot tea to enjoy on a cold morning commute when you're surrounded by your fellow travellers' coughs and sneezes.

Winter Warmer ♡

Ward off winter chills and keep colds and flu at bay with this nourishing and divinely warming tea. Ginger, cinnamon, liquorice, peppermint and star anise give it a sweet, slightly spiced flavour while quietly stimulating your defences, and echinacea gives your immune system the boost it needs. Avoid this tea if you have high blood pressure.

MAKES 1 MUGFUL

1 teaspoon dried chopped echinacea root

1 teaspoon dried peppermint

1cm piece of dried liquorice root

1cm piece of fresh root ginger, peeled and thinly sliced

1 star anise

Manuka honey, to taste

5cm cinnamon stick, to garnish (optional)

Put the herbs and spices in a large warmed teapot. Bring a kettle of filtered water to just below boiling point and pour 300ml into the teapot, then replace the teapot lid. Leave to steep for 5–10 minutes, giving the brew a quick stir from time to time. Strain the tea into a mug and stir in a little honey. Garnish with a cinnamon stick, if desired – it makes the ideal flavour-imbuing stirrer.

Ah-tea-shoo! ♡

Summer days are made for fun with friends and chilling out. If a trip to the park means snuffles, sneezes and itchy eyes for you, this refreshing drink will have you gambolling through the long grass once more. All of these herbs work to regulate the immune system and ease symptoms to keep hay fever at bay. This infusion can be enjoyed hot or cold.

MAKES 2 CUPS

1 teaspoon dried elderflower

1 teaspoon dried nettle leaf

1 teaspoon dried eyebright

½ teaspoon dried goldenrod

¼ teaspoon dried spearmint or a few fresh leaves, lightly crushed

1 slice of lemon per serving, to garnish

Put all the herbs in a warmed teapot. Bring a kettle of filtered water to just below boiling point and pour 400ml into the teapot, then replace the teapot lid. Leave to infuse for 5–10 minutes, then strain into 2 cups and garnish each cup with a slice of lemon.

Lionheart Tea

The herbs in this tea have been used traditionally to protect and support the heart and blood vessels. Hawthorn is widely used to treat early stage heart disease and to encourage the health of your circulatory system. It is helpful for angina, high blood pressure and overall heart health, too! A tasty daily cup will have benefits for everyone, especially older folk.

MAKES 1 MUGFUL

2 teaspoons dried hawthorn leaves and flowers

2 teaspoons dried linden flowers

2 teaspoons dried motherwort

1 teaspoon dried yarrow

Drop the herbs into a warmed teapot. Bring a kettle of filtered water to just below boiling point and pour 300ml into the teapot, then replace the teapot lid. Leave to steep for 10 minutes to allow the dried berries to soften and plump up. You can extract the maximum flavour and goodness from them by gently squashing the berries against the side of the pot using a spoon or fork. Strain into a mug and enjoy while it's hot.

HEALING HERBS

Many people find that hawthorn can help in heart disease and high blood pressure, but it is important to remember these are serious health issues and you should always consult a doctor before self-treating.

Aptogenius Tea ♥ ◐

Herbalists use the word 'adaptogen' to describe those herbs that help the body and mind deal with stress. These herbs contain compounds that relax and invigorate, depending upon what is required. This deeply nourishing blend helps you to adapt to stressful situations when exhaustion threatens, to help maintain wellness. This tea benefits from a longer infusing time to help the hard roots give up all their goodness. Gently crushing them in a pestle and mortar isn't strictly necessary, but will help, too. This tea is best avoided if you have an overactive thyroid or high blood pressure.

MAKES 2 CUPS

1 teaspoon dried chopped
ashwagandha root

½ teaspoon dried chopped liquorice root

1 teaspoon dried chopped rhodiola root

1 teaspoon dried gotu kola

¼ teaspoon dried chopped ginger or
5mm piece of fresh root ginger, chopped

dairy or almond milk, to taste (optional)

Crush the herbs using a pestle and mortar and put them in a warmed teapot. Bring a kettle of filtered water to just below boiling point and pour 400ml into the teapot, then replace the teapot lid. Leave to steep for at least 10 minutes, then strain into 2 cups. You can drink this infusion as it is or add a little dairy or almond milk, if liked.

HEALING HERBS

Ashwagandha is sometimes known as Indian ginseng and is traditionally prepared in India by cooking it in milk or ghee, as the fats help to release the herb's healing constituents.

Super-soothing Cough Tea ♥◐

This versatile blend can be drunk as a tea or you can increase the honey to thicken it and create a cough syrup that will keep in the refrigerator for a few days. It can help to soothe a chesty cough in adults and also in children, who will love the sweet taste. All of these herbs work on the respiratory tract and many are antiviral and antibacterial, too! Avoid drinking this tea if you have high blood pressure.

MAKES 1 MUGFUL OR ABOUT 400ML, DEPENDING ON HOW MUCH HONEY IS ADDED

1 teaspoon dried hyssop leaf

½ teaspoon dried sage

1 teaspoon dried chopped elecampane root

1 teaspoon dried mullein leaves and/or flowers

1 teaspoon dried chopped liquorice root

¼ teaspoon dried or fresh thyme

300ml filtered water

2 teaspoons to 5 tablespoons Manuka honey, depending on desired use

Put all the herbs in a small saucepan with the measured water. Bring the mixture to the boil, then reduce the heat to a low setting and simmer, uncovered, for 10 minutes to allow some of the liquid to evaporate for a concentrated flavour. Turn off the heat and leave the brew to cool. This extra steeping time results in a strong tea.

Strain the cooled tea into a clean pan. Bring slowly back to simmering point, then remove from the heat and stir in the honey until dissolved. Pour the mixture into a mug and drink it hot. If you have used the greater quantity of honey to make a cough syrup, allow the mixture to cool, then transfer it to a glass jar and keep it refrigerated for up to a week – the more honey you use, the longer it will keep. Drink a small glassful a few times a day to ease a cough.

HEALING HERBS

Hyssop is an antispasmodic herb, which means it can relieve spasmodic coughs and other spasms in the respiratory system.

Fussy, Feverish Kids' Tea

*Suitable for children older than three and generally healthy, this tea is a
great alternative to an over-the-counter remedy. Catmint and linden flower help
gently break a fever, while peppermint and chamomile soothe and relax. Liquorice
is antiviral and, along with the honey, gives the tea a sweetness that will appeal to
even the fussiest child. Avoid drinking this tea if you have high blood pressure.*

MAKES 1 CUP

1 teaspoon dried catmint leaf

1 teaspoon dried chamomile flowers

½ teaspoon dried linden flowers

½ teaspoon dried peppermint

½ teaspoon dried chopped
liquorice root

½–1 teaspoon Manuka honey

Put all the herbs in a warmed teapot. Bring a kettle of
filtered water to just below boiling point and pour 200ml
into the teapot, then replace the teapot lid. Leave the tea
to steep for at least 10 minutes, then strain into a cup.
Stir in the honey while the tea is hot, then allow to it cool –
you can add a couple of ice cubes to cool it more quickly.

TEA TIP
*If your little one is reluctant to drink this as a tea, either hot
or cold, why not freeze it in ice-lolly moulds, adding a few fresh
vitamin C-rich berries for colour and flavour?*

Conval-essence

*Our grandparents' generation believed in taking time after an illness to
rebuild strength. This tea is inspired by that idea. It blends nourishing nettle,
anti-inflammatory meadowsweet, St John's wort to counter post-viral fatigue,
schisandra to build stamina and astragalus to support the immune system.
Avoid drinking this tea if you are taking antidepressant or other medication.*

MAKES 2 MUGFULS

2 teaspoons dried nettle leaf

1 teaspoon dried meadowsweet

1 teaspoon dried St John's wort

1 teaspoon dried astragalus

1 teaspoon dried schisandra berries

Put the herbs in a large warmed teapot. Bring a kettle of
filtered water to just below boiling point and pour 600ml
into the teapot, then replace the teapot lid. Leave the tea to
steep for 5 minutes, then strain. Drink 1–2 mugfuls per day
for at least a week after sickness.

When it's Flu Tea ♥◊◊

Flu, or influenza, is different from a regular head cold. Your bones and muscles ache and a high temperature can make you feel very unwell. This healing tea is bursting with herbs to ease discomfort and promote healing. Boneset eases the pain, elderberry and St John's wort fight the virus, while echinacea and andrographis boost your immune system. Elderflower is included to break your fever. Manuka honey not only makes the tea tastier, but brings its own soothing and antimicrobial qualities (see below). Avoid drinking this tea if you have high blood pressure or are taking antidepressant or other medication.

MAKES 1 LITRE

4 teaspoons dried boneset

4 teaspoons dried chopped echinacea root

4 teaspoons dried elderberry

2 teaspoons dried elderflower

2 teaspoons dried St John's wort

1 teaspoon dried andrographis

1 litre filtered water

2 teaspoons Manuka honey, or to taste

Put all the herbs in a saucepan with the measured water. Bring to just below boiling point, then reduce the heat and simmer, covered, for 10 minutes. Remove the pan from heat and strain. While the tea is still hot, stir in the honey. Drink some immediately and pour the rest into a Thermos flask so you can drink the tea throughout the day to help ease your symptoms and fight the virus.

HEALING HERBS

Any honey will sweeten a tea and add its antibacterial qualities, but honey made by bees that have fed on the Manuka plant in New Zealand has considerably more of these compounds, making it the most antimicrobial honey available.

Tea for a Head Cold ♡ ◌ ◌

Even the healthiest of us succumb to a cold every now and then. This comforting tea will not only help you to feel better, it will also support your body in fighting off the virus. Drink a nice hot cup before wrapping yourself in blankets and snuggling somewhere warm.

MAKES 2 MUGFULS

1 teaspoon dried chopped echinacea root

1 teaspoon dried elderberry

½ teaspoon dried yarrow

½ teaspoon dried peppermint

½ teaspoon cinnamon bark chips or ¼ cinnamon stick

1cm piece of fresh root ginger, chopped, or 1 teaspoon dried ginger

1–2 teaspoons honey per serving

1 slice of lemon per serving, to garnish

Put the herbs in a large warmed teapot. Bring a kettle of filtered water to just below boiling point and pour 600ml into the teapot, then replace the teapot lid. Leave the tea to steep for 5–6 minutes, then strain into 2 mugs and stir in the honey. Serve each drink garnished with a lemon slice.

HEALING HERBS

Ginger is not only warming and anti-inflammatory, helping to reduce pain and discomfort, but it also works to support your body's own defence mechanism by promoting healthy sweating.

Chapter Six

Bliss & Happiness

This collection of healing, nurturing teas is designed to lift your mood, help you to relax and enhance wellbeing on every level. Experience rejuvenated spirits, a release of tension and wonderful, restorative sleep, or drift into sweet dreams, heighten sensual feelings and raise energy levels the natural way. A few mugfuls of happiness can go a long way towards helping you achieve lingering moments of pure serenity and absolute bliss, every day.

Happy Tea

This joy-bringing blend of mood-lifting herbs is sure to put a smile on your face. Lavender is calming, while lemon balm is known for lifting the mood. Linden flowers have been used for centuries for relaxation and rejuvenation. Rose is both an antidepressant and a natural aid for restful sleep. Liquorice promotes the action of the adrenal glands, to help you through periods of anxiety and stress. This is an unbeatable blend for banishing the blues. Avoid drinking this tea if you have high blood pressure.

MAKES 2 CUPS

2 teaspoons dried lemon balm

2 teaspoons dried linden flowers

½ teaspoon dried chopped liquorice root

pinch of dried or fresh lavender flowers

pinch of dried rose petals or 3–4 fresh petals

Place the herbs in a warmed teapot. Bring a kettle of filtered water to just below boiling point and pour 400ml into the teapot, then replace the teapot lid. Leave to steep for 3–5 minutes, then strain into 2 cups and serve piping hot. Alternatively, strain the tea into a jug, leave to cool, then transfer to a glass container and chill in the refrigerator. Serve the chilled tea over ice cubes for a refreshing, beautifully uplifting summer drink. Chilled tea will keep, refrigerated, for up to 2 days.

TEA TIP

Use just a tiny bit of lavender, as too much can make the tea taste a little soapy.

Love Potion ❤

The perfect tea to share with the object of your affections. Rose is said to open the heart, while hibiscus is believed to promote loving feelings. Fennel and cardamom inspire warmth and affection, and lemon verbena lifts the mood.

MAKES 2 CUPS

1 teaspoon dried hibiscus flowers

2 teaspoons dried lemon verbena

½ teaspoon dried rose petals or 3 fresh red rose petals

½ teaspoon dried or fresh rosemary

½ teaspoon fennel seeds

1 cardamom pod

1 fresh rose petal per serving, to garnish

Put all the herbs in a small warmed teapot. Bring a kettle of filtered water to just below boiling point. Pour 400ml hot water over the herbs in the teapot and replace the teapot lid. Allow to infuse for 7–10 minutes. Strain into 2 cups. A rose petal, floated on the surface of each cup of tea, looks pretty and will add its sweet fragrance.

Vital Force Tea ❤ ⬤

Boost your vital force with this energy-boosting blend. Siberian ginseng works against fatigue, ageing and stress, and tulsi, ashwagandha and damiana relieve anxiety and encourage physical and emotional health and wellbeing. This tea is best avoided if you have an overactive thyroid.

MAKES 1 MUGFUL

1 teaspoon dried Siberian ginseng

1 teaspoon dried ashwagandha root

½ teaspoon dried tulsi (holy basil)

½ teaspoon dried damiana leaf

¼ teaspoon dried ginger or 1cm piece of fresh root ginger, finely sliced

300ml filtered water

honey, to taste (optional)

Put all the herbs (except the ginger, if you are using fresh root) in a mortar and use a pestle to break them down a little. (Alternatively, use a clean spice grinder for this job.) Transfer the herbs to a pan with the measured water and fresh ginger, if using, and bring slowly to simmering point. Simmer for 5 minutes, then remove the pan from the heat. Leave the tea to cool a little, then strain into a mug and sweeten with a little honey, if desired.

In the Mood ❤💧

When it is time for that loving feeling, share a pot of this sensual tea with
your sweetheart. Rose, jasmine, damiana and ginger are all traditional
aphrodisiacs, and stimulating Siberian ginseng delivers a little extra oomph!
Turn down the lights, pour the tea and let the mood take you wherever it will.

MAKES 2 CUPS

1 teaspoon dried Siberian ginseng

1 teaspoon dried damiana leaf

¼ teaspoon dried ginger or 1cm piece of
fresh root ginger, chopped

½ teaspoon dried rose buds or petals

½ teaspoon dried or fresh jasmine flowers

Put the Siberian ginseng, damiana and ginger in a warmed
teapot. Bring a kettle of filtered water to just below boiling
point. Pour 400ml water into the teapot, then replace the
teapot lid. Leave to infuse for 5 minutes, then add the rose
and jasmine. Allow to steep for a further 3 minutes before
straining into 2 cups.

HEALING HERBS

Fresh jasmine has a mild sedative effect that works to relax both
body and mind. Research has found that it heightens sexual desire.

Sweet Dreams Tea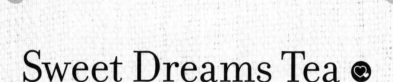

*Drifting into consciousness after a happy dream is a lovely way to start the day.
Help sweeten your dreams with a cup of this dreamy blend. Vervain relaxes
the muscles and has long been associated with deep and blissful sleep, while
chamomile and lemon balm soothe the stomach to prevent digestive discomfort
that could lead to poor sleep. This is the perfect bedtime cup of tea.*

MAKES 2 CUPS

1 teaspoon dried wood betony

1 teaspoon dried vervain leaf

1 teaspoon dried chamomile

1 teaspoon dried lemon balm

pinch of dried lavender flowers

Put all the herbs in a warmed teapot. Bring a kettle of
filtered water to just below boiling point. Pour 400ml
water into the teapot, then replace the teapot lid. Leave
to steep for 3–5 minutes, then strain into 2 cups.

TEA TIP

*Better dreams tend to come from better sleep. Why not read a book
while you enjoy this tea, rather than use a computer or phone, as the
screens can overstimulate the mind.*

Serenitea

This fragrant medley of soothing flowers encourages warmth, relaxation and balance, to help you release tension and unwind. The aromatic sweetness of liquorice provides the perfect bottom note to soothe and open your senses for a feeling of perfect harmony and absolute peace. Avoid drinking this tea if you have high blood pressure.

MAKES 2 MUGFULS

2 teaspoons dried chamomile flowers

1 teaspoon dried rose petals and buds

1 teaspoon dried calendula petals

½ teaspoon dried linden flowers and leaves

½ teaspoon dried elderflowers

2.5cm piece of dried liquorice root, chopped

½ teaspoon fennel seeds

2–3 dried lavender flowers

1 thin lemon slice, halved

Manuka honey, to taste (optional)

Put the herbs in a mortar and gently crush them with the pestle until roughly combined, then transfer to a warmed teapot. Bring a kettle of filtered water to just below boiling point, pour 600ml hot water over the herbs and replace the teapot lid. Steep for 3–5 minutes, then strain into 2 warmed, waiting mugs. Top each mugful with half a lemon slice and stir in a little nourishing honey, if desired.

TEA TIP
When hot water is added, dried flowers and leaves can swell by up to 5 times their size, so give them a nice big teapot or infuser in which to expand.

Meditation Tea

Setting aside a little time each day to meditate benefits your mind, body and spirit. This blend is designed to help focus the mind and relax the body to enhance your experience. Sip this tea before meditating. If you have high blood pressure, check with your doctor before taking rosemary in a tea, as this herb can exacerbate the condition.

MAKES 1 CUP

1 teaspoon dried tulsi (holy basil)

½ teaspoon chopped fresh rosemary

½ teaspoon dried mugwort

½ teaspoon dried vervain leaf

½ teaspoon dried rose petals

Put all the herbs and rose petals in a tea ball or infuser and place this in a cup. Bring a kettle of filtered water to just below boiling point. Pour 200ml hot water over the infuser to fill the cup. Leave to steep for 3–5 minutes, agitating the infuser from time to time, then remove the infuser.

Summer Lovin'

Cooling and light, this glorious ruby-coloured tea is always refreshing, whether it is drunk warm or chilled and served over ice. Rose, lemon verbena and hibiscus lift the heart, while spearmint, lemon grass and orange freshen and cool.

MAKES 2 MUGFULS

1 teaspoon dried hibiscus flowers

1 teaspoon dried lemon verbena

1 teaspoon dried spearmint

1 teaspoon dried chopped orange peel

½ teaspoon dried chopped lemon grass or 1cm fresh lemon grass, crushed

1 slice of orange per serving, to garnish

1 dried or fresh rose petal (preferably red or pink) per serving, to garnish

This tea looks pretty in a glass teapot with a built-in infuser — perfect for a summer party. Place the herbs inside the infuser. Bring a kettle of filtered water almost to boiling point. Pour 600ml hot water over the infuser in the warmed teapot, then replace the teapot lid. Leave to steep for 10 minutes, then strain into 2 mugs and garnish each serving with a slice of orange and a rose petal. If you are planning to serve the tea iced, leave the strained tea to cool, then refrigerate for at least 1 hour before garnishing and serving over ice.

TEA TIP

If you have borage growing nearby, pick a handful of the bright blue star-like flowers and freeze them in ice cubes. Drop the cubes into a glass jug, pour in the chilled tea and add orange slices and rose petals for a delightfully pretty summer drink.

Tea for a Broken Heart ♥

Time is the greatest healer, but herbs can help enormously during the grieving process. Hawthorn, rose and heartsease comfort the heart, while wood betony helps you regain perspective and albizia and lemon balm lift your mood. One of the loveliest things about herbs is that they work on both body and mind, and many emotional states can be healed just as easily as physical conditions.

MAKES 1 LARGE MUGFUL

1 teaspoon dried hawthorn berries

½ teaspoon dried albizia bark

300ml filtered water

1 teaspoon dried or fresh lemon balm

½ teaspoon dried wood betony

¼ teaspoon dried rosebuds or petals

¼ teaspoon dried heartsease

honey, to taste (optional)

Put the hawthorn berries and albizia bark in a small pan with the measured water. Bring to nearly boiling point, then reduce the heat and simmer for 5 minutes. Remove the pan from the heat and immediately add the remaining herbs. Cover the pan with a lid and leave the brew to steep for 10 minutes. Strain into a mug and add a little honey, if liked.

HEALING HERBS

Heartsease is also known as wild pansy, and has been traditionally used to promote good metabolism, and to ease physical and emotional fatigue among other things. It is also a wonderful natural aid to having restful, restorative sleep.

Winter Blues Tea

This rich-tasting tea has sunny St John's wort and linden flower to shine a little light into a dark winter's day, encouraging relief from symptoms of depression. Antioxidant rooibos supports your immune system, rosemary and rhodiola boost energy and a little ginger warms and comforts. Avoid drinking this tea if you are taking antidepressant or other medication.

MAKES 1 MUGFUL

1 teaspoon dried St John's wort

1 teaspoon dried rooibos

1 teaspoon dried linden flowers

½ teaspoon dried rosemary

½ teaspoon dried chopped rhodiola root

¼ teaspoon dried ginger or 1cm piece of fresh root ginger, chopped

Put all the herbs in a warmed teapot. Bring a kettle of filtered water almost to boiling point. Pour 300ml hot water into the teapot, then replace the teapot lid. Leave to steep for 5–6 minutes, then strain into a mug. This tea is most effective if you have 1–2 mugfuls each morning.

HEALING HERBS

St John's wort has been shown across a multitude of studies to ease mild to moderate depression and its associated symptoms of anxiety, sleeplessness, lack of appetite and fatigue.

Holiday Celebration Tea

*Deliciously rich and spicy, this is a lusciously fruity tea with a surge
of vitamin C and lots of antioxidants and spices, to help you digest all that
lovely food you have enjoyed over the festive period. It is perfect to share
when you are celebrating — and a dose of good health goes well with good
cheer! Avoid drinking this tea if you have high blood pressure.*

MAKES 2 MUGFULS

1 teaspoon dried hawthorn berries

1 teaspoon dried chopped liquorice root

1 teaspoon dried chopped marshmallow root

1 teaspoon dried elderberries

1 teaspoon dried rosehips

½ teaspoon coriander seeds

½ teaspoon dried chopped cinnamon
or ½ cinnamon stick, broken

600ml filtered water

2 teaspoons honey per serving, or to taste

1 cinnamon stick per serving, to garnish

Mix the herbs well and gently crush them using a pestle
and mortar. Put them in a pan with the measured water.
Heat until the water is just bubbling, then reduce the heat
and simmer for 10 minutes. Strain into 2 mugs and add the
honey, then pop a cinnamon stick stirrer into each mug.

HEALING HERBS
*Recent research has found that marshmallow root is effective
in the treatment of heartburn, indigestion, stomach ulcers and
even colitis. It also helps to balance blood sugar levels — perfect
after overindulging!*

Chapter Seven

Beyond Tea

While delightful herbal teas can address both emotional and physical health, set you on the road to recovery, ease symptoms and encourage your spirit to soar, there are other ways in which you can benefit from herbs. In this chapter you will find a cornucopia of delicious herbal extras, including gorgeous Golden Milk with turmeric, nourishing Almond Milk, fresh Flower Garden Tea to support health, a fragrant cordial and smoothie, warm, spicy herb cocoa and exquisitely flavoured healing honeys. Divine!

Chai Honey

Honey has a unique blend of antibacterial and health-boosting compounds that make it a medicine in its own right. It is easy to make your own herbal honeys to add instant flavour and medicinal actions to your tea. This chai-inspired honey contains the powdered herbs and spices that are used to create the famous Indian brew. With regular stirring, these infuse the honey. Use it to create a delicious instant chai. Just stir a spoonful or two into warmed milk, non-dairy milk or even plain hot water for a satisfying and medicinal drink.

MAKES 250G

250g jar of wildflower honey

1 teaspoon ground cinnamon

1 teaspoon ground cardamom

½ teaspoon ground ginger

½ teaspoon ground allspice

¼ teaspoon ground nutmeg

¼ teaspoon ground clove

¼ teaspoon ground coriander

Spoon 4–5 teaspoons honey out of the jar to make space for the spices and replace the lid. Stand the jar in a bowl of hot water (ensure it is not boiling water, which could crack the jar) for 5 minutes – this makes it easier to stir in the herbs. Open the lid from time to time to stir the honey a little.

Blend the spices together in a small bowl. Remove the honey from the water, dry the outside of the jar, remove the lid, then stir in the spice blend. Replace the lid and leave the jar somewhere cool and dark for at least 2 weeks to allow the spices to infuse the honey. Stir it regularly to intensify and blend the flavours. The resulting honey will keep well in a cupboard or larder, the flavour deepening over time.

TEA TIP

If you don't have powdered spices, use a pestle and mortar or a spice grinder to create a coarse powder from dried whole spices.

Healthy Honey ❤

*This delicious and versatile honey gives your immune system a fabulous kick-start.
Use it to make a quick tea by stirring a couple of spoonfuls into a mug of hot water,
or add it to winter smoothies, drizzle it over fruit or muesli, or just enjoy it spooned
straight from the jar! Avoid eating this honey if you have high blood pressure.*

MAKES 250G

4 teaspoons dried elderberries

3 teaspoons dried chopped echinacea root

1½ teaspoons dried thyme

1 teaspoon dried chopped liquorice root

½ teaspoon dried sage

1 garlic clove, finely chopped (optional)

250g jar runny wildflower honey

Combine the dried herbs well and grind them using a pestle and mortar or a clean spice grinder. Add the chopped garlic, if using, grinding it in with the herbs.

Spoon 4–5 teaspoons honey out of the jar to make space for the herbs and replace the lid. Stand the jar in a bowl of hot water (ensure it is not boiling water, which could crack the jar) for 5 minutes – this makes it easier to stir in the herbs. Open the lid from time to time to stir the honey a little.

Add the ground herbs and garlic and stir well. Replace the lid and leave the jar in a cool place out of direct light for at least 2 weeks (although it will only improve with age), stirring whenever you remember. There is no need to strain out the herbs, which is a laborious task and wastes a lot of honey. Just stir the honey before use and allow any bits to settle to the bottom of your cup if you are using the honey in a tea.

TEA TIP

*Garlic is optional in this recipe, because not everyone likes the flavour
or aroma of raw garlic, but the other herbs conceal the flavour and
garlic is an unbeatable antimicrobial ingredient. Its action will
complement that of the other herbs.*

Hot Spiced Cocoa

Chocolate is a herb too! As well as being delicious and addictive, cocoa beans are high in antioxidant polyphenols and contain mood-lifting constituents. Adding a little cayenne pepper and cardamom improves the way you digest food, making this a great drink to enjoy after a meal. When you remove or reduce the sugar, you can create your own healthy and deliciously warming hot chocolate 'tea'.

MAKES 2 MUGFULS

600ml dairy or non-dairy milk (such as almond, soya or rice milk)

4 teaspoons raw cacao powder

¼ teaspoon ground cinnamon

¼ teaspoon cayenne pepper, or to taste

½ vanilla pod

1 cardamom pod

To garnish

nutmeg

1 cinnamon stick per serving

Place the milk in a pan with the cocoa powder and spices. Warm the mixture slowly over a medium–low heat until bubbles begin to appear on the surface, then reduce the heat to the lowest setting and simmer gently for 3–5 minutes. Strain through a fine sieve into 2 mugs and serve with a little nutmeg grated over and a cinnamon stick to stir.

TEA TIP

Raw chocolate is naturally bitter, but cinnamon and vanilla add a nice sweetness. If you prefer your hot chocolate a little sweeter, add honey to taste.

Golden Milk

Delicious and comforting Golden Milk is a traditional way of serving turmeric in India, especially in the winter months. Turmeric is widely used in the Ayurvedic system of herbal medicine. Its anti-inflammatory and antimicrobial properties make it a go-to remedy for conditions from arthritis and high cholesterol to colds and flu. Check with your healthcare professional before taking this tea if you are on blood-thinning medication.

MAKES 1 MUGFUL

300ml milk (or dairy-free alternative)

1 teaspoon ground turmeric

¼ teaspoon ground cinnamon

2 black peppercorns

1 teaspoon coconut oil (optional)

honey, to taste

nutmeg, to garnish

1 cinnamon stick, to serve

Put the milk, spices and coconut oil, if using, in a pan and heat gently until the mixture almost reaches boiling point. Reduce the heat and simmer gently for 25 minutes. Take the pan off the heat and strain into a mug. Stir in honey to taste, garnish with a little grated nutmeg and serve with a cinnamon stick for stirring.

Almond Milk

This almond milk is better than anything you can buy. A powerful blender, such as a Vitamix or Nutribullet, gives the best results, but you will still get a good milk using a standard blender or a food processor with a blender attachment.

MAKES 750ML

150g whole almonds

750ml filtered water

½ teaspoon vanilla extract

3 pitted dates

¼ teaspoon ground cinnamon

pinch of sea salt

Soak the almonds overnight in filtered water. The next morning, strain and rinse the almonds, then put them in the blender with the measured water. Add the remaining ingredients and blend at maximum power for 3–5 minutes, until completely blended. Strain through a sieve lined with muslin. Squeeze out the muslin with the pulp gathered inside to extract as much liquid as possible. Transfer the almond milk to a glass container and store it in the refrigerator, where it will keep for up to 5 days. Shake before use.

Flower Garden Tea

What could be more blissful than a tea made from colourful petals plucked fresh from a flower garden? The flavonoids that give flowers their colours support the heart and cardiovascular system, while the aromatic essential oils reduce inflammation and protect from infection. Select a vibrant handful of whatever you can find from the flowers listed below and enjoy a unique and fragrant cup of tea! Flower petals are so delicate that they quickly infuse hot water, so here we reverse the usual tea-making process by adding the herbs to the water in the teapot rather than pouring it over them.

MAKES 2 CUPS

1 handful of a mixture of fresh viola flowers, calendula petals, borage flowers, rose petals, rosemary blossoms, red clover flowers, lavender flowers, blue cornflower heads, echinacea petals, nasturtium flowers and/ or scented geranium leaves (ideally rose- or lemon-scented)

Bring a kettle of filtered water almost to boiling point, then pour 400ml into a warmed teapot (a glass one will show off the delightful colours of the petals). Immediately add your petals and gently swirl them around in the liquid to help them sink. Leave to steep for 3–5 minutes, then pour into 2 cups. You can strain this tea, or leave the petals in and allow them to sink to the bottom of the cup.

HEALING HERBS

Rosemary promotes blood flow to the brain, which can lift the mood. It can exacerbate high blood pressure, so check with your doctor or herbalist before using it if this applies to you.

Allergy-ease Cordial

Infused cordials are a great way to enjoy the taste and medicinal benefits of herbs.
Keep this blend on hand in summer to treat hay fever and seasonal allergy symptoms.
Nettles contain antihistamines, to help reduce the allergic response, while eyebright
reduces inflammation and elderflower helps clear up sniffles. Use 50ml per 250ml
glass of water, or a half dose for children, and take no more than three glassfuls a day.

MAKES 450ML

250g organic caster sugar

250ml filtered water

4 teaspoons dried elderflower

4 teaspoons dried nettle leaf

3 teaspoons dried eyebright

2 teaspoons dried plantain leaf

1 teaspoon dried yarrow

1 teaspoon fennel seeds

lemon, for squeezing

Heat the sugar and measured water in a small saucepan over a low heat, carefully swirling the pan to help the sugar dissolve. While the sugar syrup is heating, gently crush all the herbs using a pestle and mortar. As soon as all the sugar has dissolved and you have a pan full of clear liquid, take the pan off the heat and drop all the herbs into it. Swirl once more to ensure the herbs are immersed in the syrup, then cover the pan with a tight-fitting lid and leave the herbs to infuse the syrup as it cools.

Once the syrup is completely cold, carefully strain out the herbs. Bottle and label the cordial and store it in the refrigerator, where it will keep for up to 3 weeks.

To serve, muddle 1 part cordial with 5 parts still or sparkling water. Squeeze in a little lemon juice as you serve the cordial to brighten and enhance the flavour.

TEA TIP

Although this cordial requires quite a lot of sugar to preserve it,
you will only be consuming a little each time you use it,
diluted with still or sparkling water.

Immune-boosting Smoothie 🖤

Adding the decoction below to your morning smoothie will provide it with countless medicinal benefits. Each of these herbs has a direct impact on immune system health. Use some or all of the decoction in your usual smoothie recipe, or try it with this winning smoothie, which includes anti-inflammatory pomegranate juice and antioxidant-rich blueberries.

MAKES 1 TALL GLASSFUL

For the decoction

2 teaspoons dried elderberries

2 teaspoons dried chopped echinacea root

150ml filtered water

2 teaspoons dried lemon balm

1 teaspoon dried peppermint

For the smoothie

up to 1 quantity decoction (see above)

100ml Almond Milk (see page 123)

100ml pomegranate juice

handful of fresh or frozen blueberries

½ banana

To make the decoction, heat the elderberries, echinacea and measured water in a pan over a medium heat until bubbles start to appear on the surface, then reduce the heat and simmer, uncovered, for 5 minutes, just until the berries start to burst. Take the pan off the heat and immediately add the lemon balm and peppermint. Cover the pan with a tight-fitting lid and leave the decoction to cool completely. Strain well into a jug, pressing the herbs against the side of the sieve with a spoon to extract all the goodness, then transfer to a glass bottle. Use immediately or refrigerate for up to 1 day for later use.

To make the smoothie, combine the ingredients in a blender, then pour into a tall glass.

TEA TIP

Make this decoction in the evening and refrigerate it overnight to speed up your morning routine. Or try scaling up the recipe and freezing it in an ice-cube tray. Simply add 3–4 cubes to your smoothie.

Fresh Herb Sorbet

A beautiful way to capture the flavour and medicinal qualities of fresh summer herbs is to create a sorbet. You can experiment with your own combinations, but the herbs below all contain mood-lifting properties and make a beautiful pale-green delight that is divinely refreshing and cooling.

SERVES 6–8

250g caster sugar

5–10g combination of fresh herbs, such as rose geranium leaves, lemon verbena, rose petals, mint and lemon balm (the exact weight will vary according to the herbs you choose, but aim to have enough to loosely fill a teacup)

750ml filtered water

juice of 1 lemon

In a food processor, blend the sugar and herbs together until they form a thick paste, scraping down any mixture that gets caught on the sides of the bowl. Add about 100ml of the measured water and purée again. Add the remaining measured water and lemon juice and blend once more until the mixture is fully combined. Chill in the refrigerator for at least 2 hours, then freeze in an ice-cream maker according to the manufacturer's instructions. (Alternatively, simply pour the mixture into a wide, flat container, then freeze it, taking it out of the freezer to give it a vigorous stirring every couple of hours while it sets.)

TEA TIP

A few leaves of anise hyssop make a lovely addition to this blend, and they are gorgeously aromatic in teas, too. Check seed catalogues and nurseries to find a plant.

Ashwagandha and Turmeric Colada ❤️ 💊

*Drinking this delicious mocktail is a great way to enjoy the benefits of ashwagandha,
the famed Indian herb that strengthens the adrenal glands and calms the spirit.
Turmeric boosts immunity and reduces inflammation. Both herbs extract best into a
liquid with a higher fat content, making coconut milk the perfect choice for this exotic
beverage. The pineapple helps to support digestion and coconut milk offers great-quality
protein and essential fatty acids. Avoid this drink if you have an overactive thyroid and
check with your doctor before taking it if you are on blood-thinning medication.*

MAKES 2 TALL GLASSFULS

300ml organic coconut milk

3 teaspoons powdered ashwagandha

½ teaspoon ground turmeric

250ml pineapple juice

4 ice cubes

fresh pineapple wedge per serving,
to garnish

Empty the coconut milk into a lidded jar and add the
ashwagandha and turmeric. Shake well and refrigerate
for at least 30 minutes.

When you are ready to make the colada, put the infused
coconut milk, pineapple juice and ice cubes in a blender
or liquidizer and blend until smooth. Pour the colada
into attractive glasses and garnish each with a pineapple
wedge. A little paper umbrella is entirely optional!

KEY TO INGREDIENTS

avoid when breastfeeding

avoid when taking medication
(which is specified, where appropriate)

avoid during pregnancy

[ ]

conditions in which the herb
is contraindicated

It is important to consult your doctor or a qualified herbalist before self-medicating with any herbs, particularly if you are pregnant, breastfeeding, have a health condition or are taking medication.

Herb-pedia

Most herbs have properties that provide a wealth of benefits to health and wellbeing. Below are listed just some of the qualities of the herbs that are used to make the delicious teas in this book.

AGRIMONY *Agrimonia eupatoria*
All parts of this beautiful herb can be used therapeutically to treat conditions such as digestive problems, diarrhoea, cystitis, bloating, liver problems, rheumatism and skin problems such as eczema and acne.

ALBIZIA BARK/FLOWERS
Albizia julibrissin ♡
Albizia is known as the tree of happiness and has been used traditionally to relieve anxiety, depression and the symptoms of stress. Widely used in Chinese medicine, it can also help with insomnia, memory problems, pain, some allergic disorders, swelling and circulatory problems.

ALLSPICE *Pimenta dioica* ♡
Used to prevent and treat flatulence, vomiting, indigestion, diarrhoea and other digestive problems, allspice can also stimulate appetite and support the nervous system. It is a natural remedy for fevers, menstrual cramps and joint pain.

ANDROGRAPHIS
Andrographis paniculata ♡
Known for its immune-stimulating properties, this bitter herb can help to prevent and fight viruses, fungi and bacterial infections. It also promotes digestive health, supports the liver, eases high blood pressure and acts as an anti-inflammatory.

ANGELICA ROOT
Angelica archangelica ♡ ◯ ◉
[blood-thinning medication]
Traditionally used to bring down a fever and treat coughs, colds and lung conditions, this herb can also support the urinary tract and heart, ease rheumatism and fight bacterial infections. It's also rich in nutrients that support health on all levels.

ANISEED *Pimpinella anisum* ♡
With its strong, characteristic flavour, this popular herb is often used to treat coughs, congestion and even asthma, as well as digestive problems, cramping, nausea, headaches, anxiety and poor appetite. There is some evidence to suggest that it can boost sex drive and also milk supply in nursing mothers.

ASHWAGANDHA *Withania somnifera* **[overactive thyoid]**
This is considered to be one of the most important and powerful herbs in Ayurvedic (traditional Indian) medicine. It helps to rejuvenate, boost energy levels, reduce fatigue and symptoms of stress, protect the immune system, balance blood sugar levels and reduce anxiety. It acts as an adaptogen (see page 93). Studies suggest that it may boost thyroid function.

ASTRAGALUS
Astragalus membranaceus ♡ ◯
[auto-immune conditions] This is used to encourage the health of the immune system, boost energy levels, treat colds, flu and the symptoms of stress. It also acts as an overall tonic. Traditionally, it is not used during the acute stage of an infection but to avoid illness and during convalescence.

BACOPA *Bacopa monnieri* ♡ ◯
Used therapeutically for millennia in Ayurvedic medicine, bacopa is said to enhance concentration and memory and encourage the health of the brain. It is also used to improve sleep, treat stress and ease anxiety.

BEARBERRY
Arctostaphylos uva-ursi ♡
This natural diuretic helps to improve the health of the bladder and kidneys,

and is often used to treat cystitis and urinary tract infections. It is also used to treat muscular and joint pain and can act as an anti-inflammatory.

BILBERRIES *Vaccinium myrtillus*

These pretty blue berries are very high in antioxidants, which help to prevent the degenerative effects of ageing. They are used therapeutically to encourage healthy circulation, strengthen blood vessels, balance blood sugar, ease diarrhoea and improve vision.

BLACK COHOSH

Cimicifuga racemosa 🖤💧
[oestrogen-sensitive conditions]
Most commonly used to treat symptoms associated with menstruation and menopause, such as mood swings, menstrual cramps and hot flushes, black cohosh is also known for the anti-inflammatory benefits it provides. It can help to ease arthritis and nerve pain.

BLACK HOREHOUND

Ballota nigra
With a well-deserved reputation for alleviating nausea and vomiting, particularly when caused by the nervous system, this is used to treat motion sickness, and nausea in early pregnancy or as a side effect of medication.

BLACK PEPPERCORNS

Piper nigrum
A grind of pepper enhances any meal, but it is more than just a flavourful condiment. The warming, spicy oils in black pepper help the body more effectively absorb and use the active ingredients in many other herbs, particularly those such as turmeric, which extract best into an oily medium. The herb also supports good digestion, reducing gas and easing inflammation.

BLACKBERRY LEAF

Rubus villosus
There is a host of therapeutic uses for this common antioxidant-rich herb, including the treatment of diarrhoea, sore throats, mouth ulcers and inflamed gums, and is used to attack the bacteria that cause ulcers. Blackberry leaf tea is a traditional cough remedy.

BLUE FLAG ROOT *Iris versicolor*
🖤💧✦ [blood-thinning medication; digoxin] In small doses, blue flag is an excellent detoxifier and encourages the health of the liver. It is commonly used to treat skin problems such as eczema and acne, and can help with stress, headaches, constipation and bloating.

BONESET *Eupatorium perfoliatum*
🖤💧 Both the leaves and the flowers of this herb can be used to treat colds and fever and to boost immunity. It is particularly useful as a flu remedy as it reduces the muscle and bone pain that can accompany true influenza. It also acts as a laxative, has antibacterial and painkilling properties, and is particularly useful for relieving migraines and muscular cramps and pain.

BORAGE *Borago officinalis* 🖤
Also known as starflower, borage has a traditional association with courage and strength. It is often used to treat the symptoms of stress, and it acts as an overall tonic. Borage can also be helpful for depression and irritability associated with menopause and menstruation.

BUCHU *Barosma betulina* 🖤
With a delicious blackcurrant taste, which has led to it being used as a natural flavouring, buchu is both a natural diuretic (making it useful for urinary tract infections and cystitis) and an anti-inflammatory that can be used to ease overindulgence, gout, arthritis and rheumatism. It is also traditionally used as an overall tonic to promote good health.

BURDOCK *Arctium lappa* 🖤💧
[allergy to daisy-family plants]
Burdock is a diuretic and laxative herb that can promote the health of the urinary and digestive systems and, through that, it helps with skin complaints such as acne and eczema. It has been used successfully to balance blood sugar levels and it also has antibacterial and anti-inflammatory properties.

CALENDULA *Calendula officinalis*
[allergy to daisy-family plants]
The flowers of this plant have many uses, such as to ease inflammation and encourage skin health, including treating eczema and acne. This herb boosts the lymphatic system so is good after infections and for water retention. It is an effective antifungal, used to treat thrush and other fungal infections, and can be used as a mouthwash for oral infections.

CALIFORNIA POPPY

Eschscholzia californica 🖤💧
This pretty flower has a huge number of therapeutic qualities – it supports the nervous system, reduces symptoms of stress and anxiety, encourages healthy sleep patterns, reduces fever, eases pain and tension, and acts as an antispasmodic and antihistamine.

CARAWAY SEEDS *Carum carvi* 🖤
Particularly effective on the digestive system, caraway helps to relieve colic (including in babies), flatulence and discomfort. It can also be used to bring down a fever, treat coughs and ease pain.

CARDAMOM

Elettaria cardamomum 🖤
This Eastern spice has long been used to treat urinary tract infections, high cholesterol, digestive problems, low libido and poor circulation. It has also been used as an antidepressant.

CATMINT LEAVES *Nepeta cataria* 🖤
Catmint (also known as catnip) has traditionally been used to ease fever, colds and flu, for which it makes a safe and effective remedy for children. It promotes the health of the digestive system and is used to treat diarrhoea, vomiting and flatulence. Headaches, symptoms of stress, arthritis and irregular periods are also treated with this gentle herb.

CAYENNE PEPPER

Capsicum annuum 🖤💧
[blood-thinning medication]
This powerful spice is often used for detoxification and to stimulate circulation and digestion. It has been used to treat fevers, sore throats, joint pain, colds and flu, and may help to prevent migraines. It is also an anti-allergen, and can ease symptoms and boost immunity.

CELERY SEED *Apium graveolens* ♥
In Ayurvedic medicine, celery seeds are used to treat colds, flu, liver congestion and disease, arthritis and digestive problems, while Western herbalists prescribe them for nervous disorders, inflammation, arthritis and high blood pressure. This herb is always included in herbal prescriptions for gout, as it helps to break down the crystalline deposits that cause this painful joint condition.

CHAMOMILE *Matricaria recutita*
[allergy to daisy-family plants]
Everyone is aware of the soothing effect of a cup of chamomile tea, and it can be used to relieve insomnia, reduce the effects of stress, ease anxiety and encourage healthy digestion (it is used to treat diarrhoea and relieve colic in babies). It may also help to relieve menstrual cramps and keep periods regular. Strong chamomile tea is an effective remedy for a stress headache.

CHASTE TREE BERRIES
Vitex agnus-castus ♥ [oestrogen-sensitive conditions] These small brown berries are widely used to balance hormones, to treat menstrual and menopausal symptoms including mood swings, hot flushes, breast tenderness and more. It can also be used to encourage milk supply in nursing mothers and to treat acne and excessive hair growth caused by Polycystic Ovarian Syndrome (PCOS).

CHICORY ROOT *Cichorium intybus* ♥ [allergy to daisy-family plants]
This herb can be used to encourage healthy digestion, reduce pain caused by arthritis and other inflammatory conditions, boost immunity, fight bacteria and promote heart health. It is also used for detoxification, and it can support the liver and gallbladder.

CINNAMON
Cinnamomum zeylanicum ♥
This spice is useful in the treatment of blood sugar imbalances, digestive disturbances (including diarrhoea and vomiting) and inflammatory conditions such as arthritis. It may also promote the health of the brain.

CLEAVERS *Galium aparine*
[allergy to daisy-family plants]
As a natural diuretic, cleavers can not only ease water retention and act as a detoxifier, but can also help to treat urinary tract infections. Some research suggests that it can reduce blood pressure and improve skin conditions, such as acne and psoriasis.

CLOVES *Syzygium aromaticum* ♥
Cloves are used to treat inflammation of the joints and as an analgesic for tooth and gum pain. In Ayurvedic medicine, they are used to prevent and treat colds and flu, and to expel mucus. They may also encourage healthy digestion.

CORIANDER SEEDS
Coriandrum sativum ♥
Coriander is not just a culinary spice. These seeds aid digestion and promote the healthy function of the liver, balance blood sugar levels, fight unhealthy bacteria and detoxify the body. They can also be used for eye disease and problems such as conjunctivitis.

CORN SILK *Zea mays*
Corn silk tea has been drunk for millennia by Native Americans, and today it is most commonly used as a soothing diuretic and in the treatment of urinary tract infections, acting both to treat inflammation and attack bacteria. It also gently lowers blood pressure and promotes healthy circulation.

COUCH GRASS *Agropyron repens*
A natural diuretic and antibiotic, this herb is ideal for problems associated with the urinary tract. It can also help to ease and treat a sore throat and it works as an expectorant to clear mucus from the airways. As a detoxifier, it offers support to both kidneys and liver.

CRAMP BARK *Viburnum opulus*
As the name suggests, this woody herb is most commonly used to treat cramps, particularly menstrual cramps, although it is effective throughout the body. It has been used in the treatment of migraines, headaches, mild asthma and IBS, and can promote heart health and help to balance blood pressure.

DAMIANA *Turnera diffusa* ♥
This Mexican herb has been used for centuries in the treatment of low libido and as a digestive aid. As a tonic, it boosts energy by improving the flow of oxygenated blood around the body. It has a mildly stimulant effect, making it a useful energy booster.

DANDELION *Taraxacum officinale*
[allergy to daisy-family plants]
Both the leaves and the roots of these common herbs (not weeds!) have been used to treat a huge range of health conditions, including poor liver function, constipation, skin problems, weight loss, urinary problems and blood sugar imbalances, including diabetes. The leaves are a natural, powerful diuretic, used to reduce water retention. The range of effects on the liver, bowel and urinary system makes it an effective detoxifier.

DEVIL'S CLAW
Harpagophytum procumbens ♥ ♦
[heart conditions] A strong painkiller and anti-inflammatory, devil's claw is used widely for arthritis, and pain in the joints, lower back, knee, hips and muscles. It is also used for digestive disorders, to stimulate poor appetite to help bring down a fever.

DILL SEEDS *Anethum graveolens* ♥
The flavourful seeds of this common garden herb deliver a host of benefits – they help to improve digestion and ease digestive complaints, insomnia, and menstrual and respiratory problems. It may also help to balance blood sugar levels and improve immune function.

ECHINACEA *Echinacea angustifolia/purpurea* ♥
[allergy to daisy-family plants]
Both the flowers and the roots of this plant are used therapeutically, and their prime, well-documented action is stimulating the immune system to fight off infection. Colds, flu and other viruses will all respond if echinacea is taken at the first sign of illness. There is also some evidence that it can encourage wound healing and reduce inflammation associated with skin problems and even arthritis.

ELDERBERRIES *Sambucus nigra* 🖤
This antioxidant-rich, tasty berry has been shown in a number of studies to be one of the most antiviral substances available to us. As well as preventing and fighting viral infections, these berries encourage eye and heart health and boost immunity. They can also be used in the treatment of hay fever and other allergic illnesses.

ELDERFLOWERS *Sambucus nigra*
A common sight in the English countryside, elderflower has plenty of health benefits and is renowned for its anti-inflammatory properties. It is commonly used for respiratory conditions, such as colds, flu, coughs and sinus problems, and its antibacterial and antiviral qualities make it ideal for treating allergies and supporting the immune system.

ELECAMPANE *Inula helenium*
[allergy to daisy-family plants]
A widely used herb for thousands of years, elecampane is primarily known for its effect on the respiratory system, helping to ease asthma, coughs, colds and lung infections. It also boosts the overall health of the digestive system. It contains substances known as prebiotics, which may promote a good balance of digestive bacterial flora.

EYEBRIGHT *Euphrasia officinalis*
This herb has long been used to treat eye problems and to encourage the overall health of the eyes. It does, however, also boost the respiratory system and ease breathing problems associated with hay fever, asthma, inflammation and infection.

FENNEL SEED
Foeniculum vulgare 🖤
With a distinctive liquorice taste, these little seeds pack a powerful punch in reducing digestive gas and bloating. They are also used in cough medicines and for sore throats. They are an excellent choice for breastfeeding mums, as they help to increase the flow of breast milk, and their properties travel through breast milk to gently ease a baby's colic.

FENUGREEK
Trigonella foenum-graecum 🖤
Best known as an important flavouring in Indian cuisine, these oddly shaped little seeds safely and effectively increase milk production in breastfeeding mothers. Fenugreek is also used in the form of a gargle for sore throats and is taken for bronchitis.

FEVERFEW
Tanacetum parthenium 🖤 💧
[allergy to daisy-family plants]
The leaves and daisy-like flowers of this herb are widely used to prevent and treat migraine and headaches. Feverfew is also used to address other inflammatory conditions of the head, including tinnitus and dizziness.

FIGWORT *Scrophularia nodosa* 🖤
[rapid heartbeat (tachycardia)]
Named for its tiny fig-like fruit, this herb is commonly found growing wild. The leaves and stalks are used to treat itchy and congested skin conditions, helping to support detoxification through the kidneys and digestive system.

GINGER *Zingiber officinale*
Aromatic and warming, ginger stimulates the digestive system to support good digestion. Its antimicrobial qualities make it useful for colds and flu, with the added benefit of inducing sweating. Traditionally seen as an aphrodisiac.

GINGKO LEAF *Gingko biloba*
💧 [blood thinning medication]
By increasing circulation, the leaves of this ancient tree are said to help to improve memory and mental function. Its stimulating effects on the venous blood system may also benefit those with pain or weakness in their lower legs due to poor circulation.

GOATS' RUE *Galega officinalis* 🖤
With its pink pea-like flowers, goats' rue is a common sight in summer meadows in Britain. It is popular with diabetics and people who suffer from fluctuating blood sugar levels, as research has shown it can help to balance blood sugar. It is also used by breastfeeding mums to help increase milk supply.

GOLDENROD *Solidago virgaurea*
[allergy to daisy-family plants]
The go-to herb for catarrh and nasal congestion caused by colds or hay fever, and for sinus problems. An infusion of this herb also makes an effective gargle for laryngitis and pharyngitis. As a diuretic and urinary antiseptic, it has been used to reduce the symptoms of cystitis and urinary infections.

GOTU KOLA *Centella asiatica* 🖤 💧 💧
This herb has been used for thousands of years in India and China to treat varicose veins and for its ability to improve memory and mental clarity. It helps reduce anxiety and, as an adaptogen, it helps reduce the effects of stress on the body. Used externally, it stimulates wound healing and prevents infection.

HAWTHORN *Crataegus laevigata*
💧 [heart and blood pressure medication] The leaves and flowers as well as the berries of this small tree in the rose family are used to support good function of the heart and cardiovascular system. Studies have shown that it can reduce blood pressure by strengthening arterial walls and that regular use may help the heart function more effectively. It is also used by herbalists who work with plant 'energetics' (the idea that plants work on a spiritual as well as physical level) to help support people in times of grief.

HEARTSEASE *Viola tricolor*
The delightful flowers of this wild cousin of the pansy are harvested along with the leaves and taken as an anti-inflammatory expectorant for coughs and bronchitis. It is often taken for weeping eczema and other skin problems, as well as for cystitis and other bladder infections. Traditionally it was seen to represent love and features in the love potion in Shakespeare's *A Midsummer Night's Dream*.

HIBISCUS FLOWERS
Hibiscus rosa-sinensis
As well as lending their vibrant ruby-red colour to infusions, hibiscus flowers are an excellent source of vitamin C. They have a delightfully refreshing, sour, fruity taste and have traditionally been used for colds and flu in the Middle East. Several studies in Iran suggest they may help to normalize blood pressure.

HOP FLOWERS *Humulus lupulus*
💗⊘ [antidepressants; oestrogen-sensitive conditions] Also known as strobiles, the female flowers of hop are best known for flavouring and preserving beer. They are a powerful sedative, promoting deep sleep and calming intense anxiety, and can be taken as a tea as well as used to stuff a herbal sleep pillow. They have also been used by women as an aphrodisiac. They are traditionally avoided when treating people suffering from depression.

HORSETAIL *Equisetum arvense* 💗
[long-term use; alcoholism] With its bottlebrush stems, this is one of our oldest surviving plants, having been a food source for the dinosaurs. It is an effective diuretic that is used to treat bladder conditions such as cystitis, and its reputation for toning the bladder has resulted in its use for urinary incontinence and an enlarged prostate.

HYSSOP *Hyssopus officinalis* 💗
The essential oils in this fragrant herb reduce spasms, especially in coughs and lung problems. It is helpful in colds and other respiratory infections and, with its calming and relaxing properties, makes a safe and effective remedy for children suffering from winter viruses.

JAMAICAN DOGWOOD
Piscidia erythrina 💗
Best used in small quantities, Jamaican dogwood is a powerful muscle relaxant, used to alleviate menstrual and digestive cramps. When insomnia is due to nervous tension and pain, it combines well with sedative herbs to induce deep and refreshing sleep. (This herb is toxic to fish so should be kept away from them.)

JASMINE FLOWERS
Jasminum officinale 💗
With their intoxicating fragrance, jasmine flowers have long been associated with love and passion. The sweet smell has numerous aromatherapeutic benefits to the nervous system, including lifting mood and inducing a calm, relaxed state.

LADY'S MANTLE
Alchemilla mollis 💗
There is nothing prettier on a summer's morning than silver droplets of dew held in the folds of this herb's pale green leaves. Indeed, the alchemists prized such dew highly, believing it held magical properties, which inspired the plant's botanical name, *Alchemilla*. Lady's mantle has a special affinity with the uterus and helps to reduce excessive menstrual bleeding and ease period pain. Its astringency may also help in a mouthwash to treat mouth ulcers and as a gargle for sore, inflamed throats.

LAVENDER
Lavandula angustifolia
Nothing says summer like the fragrant purple spikes of lavender flowers. Lavender is rightly famed for its ability to calm the nervous system. A little added to an infusion will help relax the mind and improve sleep as well as reduce muscle tension and spasms.

LEMON BALM *Melissa officinalis*
Although it looks like its cousin mint, the distinctive citrus scent of lemon balm is unmistakable. It not only makes a delicious tea but is unbeatable for lifting mood and alleviating feelings of stress and tension. Studies suggest that this herb may help maintain good memory into old age and confirm its antiviral qualities, making it an ideal choice when winter viruses threaten.

LEMON VERBENA
Aloysia citrodora
With its sparkling lemony taste, an infusion of this herb is refreshing and cooling when drunk cold on a summer's day. It has a reputation for raising the spirits and supporting deep, restful sleep.

LEMON GRASS
Cymbopogon citratus
A staple of Asian cuisine, this herb is also widely used in India to treat coughs and relieve nasal congestion. In the West, it is often used to treat high blood pressure, aching joints, fever, digestive problems and vomiting.

LINDEN FLOWER
Tilia × europaea
The flower of the linden tree is also known as lime flower and in France, *tilleul*. This sweetly fragrant herb has an impressive range of medicinal benefits. Tea made using linden flowers is an effective remedy for fever, and is suitable for children as well as adults – its calming and relaxing properties will help settle even the fussiest child. It is also considered a tonic for the circulatory system, reducing blood cholesterol levels and normalizing blood pressure.

LIQUORICE ROOT
Glycyrrhiza glabra 💗⊘ [high blood pressure; kidney disease; oestrogen-sensitive conditions]
Liquorice has been prized for millennia for its innumerable medicinal benefits and sweet taste. It helps relieve a chesty cough by moving trapped phlegm and soothing soreness, while its antiviral properties help with viruses. An effective anti-inflammatory, liquorice can ease digestive inflammation and other inflammatory conditions. A member of the pea family, it contains phyto-oestrogens, which can treat and prevent many of the symptoms of menopause.

MARSHMALLOW LEAF AND ROOT *Althaea officinalis*
Both root and leaf of the marshmallow plant are high in soothing, cooling mucilage (see page 47). They may be used interchangeably, although traditionally, the root is used to soothe digestive inflammation and urinary infections, while the leaf is used to treat sore throats, coughs and chest infections.

MEADOWSWEET
Filipendula ulmaria [aspirin allergy]
The grassy green aroma of an infusion of meadowsweet is reminiscent of lying in

a summer meadow. It has a well-deserved reputation as a healer of heartburn and excess digestive acidity. It is also rich in anti-inflammatory salicylates, the active ingredient in aspirin (which gets its name from the old botanical name for meadowsweet, *Spiraea ulmaria*) and so is an effective herb to use in arthritis and inflammatory conditions to reduce inflammation and ease pain.

MILK THISTLE *Carduus marianus*
[allergy to daisy-family plants; oestrogen-sensitive conditions]
The tiny hard seeds of this thistle plant need to be ground or crushed before use. Numerous studies have confirmed how helpful they can be in supporting and detoxifying the liver, speeding up the rate at which liver cells are produced and so increasing liver function. The white lines that marble the plant's leaves were once seen as divine confirmation of its other major action, which is to increase milk production in breastfeeding mothers.

MOTHERWORT *Leonorus cardiaca*
[heart disease, unless under practitioner supervision]
This herb has traditionally been used in folk medicine to support mothers and people who need 'mothering'. It is an effective and gentle remedy for anxiety and tension, particularly during times of change such as the menopause. It is considered a tonic for the heart and often used when nerves cause palpitations that are not due to heart disease.

MUGWORT *Artemisia vulgaris*
[allergy to daisy-family plants]
Mugwort is a member of the Artemisia family, from where it gets its bitter and aromatic character. As a bitter, it stimulates appetite and digestive function, helping the body to extract maximum nutrition from food and relieve any discomfort after overindulging. The herb has a traditional association with protection and dreaming. It has been strung around doors and taken before bed to promote lucid dreaming.

NETTLE LEAF *Urtica dioica*
A greedy feeder that is highly efficient at extracting nutrients from the soil, nettle leaves are high in minerals, making them a good choice for nursing mothers and in convalescence. Antihistamine constituents help reduce the symptoms and discomfort of hay fever and seasonal allergies, while their detoxifying effect can help to relieve itchy skin conditions such as eczema.

OAT SEEDS *Avena sativa*
These milky seeds are better known for their role in your morning porridge, but oat seed is also a useful and effective medicinal herb. Considered strengthening for the whole nervous system, it helps speed recovery after illness, alleviate exhaustion and calm the senses during times of stress and anxiety.

OREGANO *Origanum vulgare*
The small leaves of this plant, which is also known as marjoram, are packed with flavour and widely used to enhance sauces and stews. Oregano is an effective antiseptic and is used for mouthwashes and gargles, and can help to relieve coughs as well as headaches. The oil found in the plant has antifungal properties that make it a helpful herb for candida infections and in conditions such as ringworm and cradle cap.

OREGON GRAPE ROOT *Berberis aquifolium*
Sometimes described as the natural antibiotic, this herb has powerful bacteria-fighting properties and is excellent as a wash or gargle for tooth and throat infections, and as an antiseptic for external use. It is widely used to treat skin conditions such as acne and psoriasis, for which its efficacy is due to its stimulating and supportive action on the liver and gall bladder. It is a good gentle laxative for occasional use.

PARSLEY *Petroselinum crispum*
Both the curly and flat-leaved varieties of parsley are effective diuretics, helping to flush away excess water. It also makes a useful after-dinner herb, freshening the breath and reducing feelings of excessive gas and bloating. The fresh leaves are a rich source of vitamin C.

PASSIONFLOWER *Passiflora incarnata*
This exotic-looking flower has hypnotic qualities. It has been used to treat insomnia and ensure a deep and easy sleep. In smaller quantities, it reduces anxiety and tension during the day, too, and was traditionally used to treat hysteria and seizures. It has been widely used to treat nerve pain and neuralgia and as part of a remedy for asthma.

PEPPERMINT *Mentha × piperita*
Cooling and refreshing peppermint makes the perfect after-dinner tea, which helps to relieve indigestion and support good digestion. It is excellent for reducing excess gas and may help in the treatment of more serious digestive ailments such as ulcerative colitis. As a source of menthol, it is helpful in a hot tea to relieve nasal congestion in colds and sinus infections. Peppermint may also help to settle the stomach in motion sickness and nausea.

PLANTAIN *Plantago lanceolata*
Not to be confused with the banana-like vegetable from the Caribbean, this humble leafy plant can be found worldwide near human habitation. It is an excellent source of mucilages (gloopy starches that soothe inflamed tissue), especially in the throat, lungs and digestive system. Helpful for hay fever and congestion, plantain also soothes after a stomach upset or food poisoning.

RASPBERRY LEAF *Rubus idaeus*
(until final trimester)
Raspberry leaves can be used for their toning effect on the uterus. Midwives recommend taking raspberry leaf tea in

the final stage of pregnancy to strengthen the uterus and prepare for childbirth. The leaves are also helpful postnatally, to help increase uterine tone.

RED CLOVER *Trifolium pratense*
[oestrogen-sensitive conditions]
Seen as a blood cleanser by traditional herbalists, the flowers and leaves are safe and effective remedies for chronic skin conditions and are particularly useful in childhood eczema. The oestrogen-like compounds found in red clover have led to suggestions that it may be helpful in reducing menopausal symptoms.

RHODIOLA *Rhodiola rosea* 💚
Renowned for its energy-boosting properties and ability to alleviate altitude sickness, rhodiola has also been shown to reduce the symptoms of mild to moderate depression. A helpful ally in times of stress, this herb helps the body resist the long-term effects of prolonged exposure to stress hormones.

RHUBARB ROOT *Rheum palmatum* 💚
Sometimes known as Turkey rhubarb, this herb is not to be confused with garden rhubarb, the roots of which are toxic. It is an effective laxative and is used to treat constipation, especially if taken in the evening.

ROOIBOS *Aspalathus linearis*
This rich-tasting South African herb makes an excellent caffeine-free alternative to black tea. It is an abundant source of antioxidant compounds, which can protect heart health and may prevent cancer and other serious diseases. It is also a good source of minerals that help to maintain bone strength and may protect against diabetes.

ROSE GERANIUM LEAVES *Pelargonium graveolens*
Scented geraniums come in a wide range of fragrances, including cinnamon, eau du cologne and even chocolate mint. One of the most popular is rose geranium, whose beautiful aroma lifts the heart and spirits. All geraniums are astringent, helping to settle digestive upsets and relieve chronic diarrhoea.

ROSE PETALS *Rosa damascena*
The renowned herbalist Christopher Hedley likens rose to 'a hug in a bottle'. While its medicinal qualities are limited to being a mild astringent, useful in upset stomachs and sore throats, it is widely prized for its ability to lift the spirits, alleviate mild depressive feelings and comfort the heart in times of sadness. Rose is also widely seen as the flower that represents love and romance.

ROSEHIPS *Rosa canina*
The scarlet berries of the wild rose have long been recognized as an excellent source of vitamin C. Teas and soups made with the dried berries were a valuable staple during the long winters in Scandinavia, when plants were scarce. Recent studies suggest that the berries have a powerful anti-inflammatory effect, particularly in reducing the pain and swelling associated with arthritis.

ROSEMARY *Rosmarinus officinalis* 💚
[high blood pressure]
Stimulating rosemary is often used to improve memory and boost energy levels. It increases blood flow around the body, boosting oxygen levels in the brain and alleviating some types of headache that are due to poor circulation.

SAGE *Salvia officinalis* 💚 💧
[oestrogen-sensitive conditions]
An infusion of sage makes an excellent gargle for sore throats, helping to fight infection and soothe swollen membranes. It can also be used to treat tooth and gum problems and mouth ulcers. Drunk cold, sage is highly effective at reducing perspiration, making it ideal for menopausal hot flushes as well as nervous sweating. Sage can reduce milk supply, so is not suitable in breastfeeding, but can be helpful when it is time to wean.

SARSAPARILLA *Smilax ornata* 💚 💧
An important herb in the treatment of skin conditions such as itchy eczema and psoriasis, sarsaparilla has the ability to improve circulation and elimination in the body. It is also used for rheumatoid arthritis and other rheumatic conditions.

SCHISANDRA BERRIES *Schisandra chinensis* 💚 💧
An important part of the Chinese *materia medica*, this adaptogenic (see page 93) berry has been used for thousands of years to extend life, slow down the process of ageing, enhance energy levels and boost libido. With its significant antioxidant and anti-inflammatory properties, it can encourage health throughout the body and it is included in blends to support emotional health.

SHATAVARI ROOT *Asparagus racemosus* 💚
Shatavari is seen primarily as a herb for women. Its name means 'woman with a hundred husbands' and refers to the way in which this herb supports female hormonal function throughout reproductive life. The herb is most commonly used to enhance fertility and has an important role to play in menopause, helping to control symptoms such as hot flushes.

SIBERIAN GINSENG *Eleutherococcus senticosus* 💚 💧
[high blood pressure] One of the best-known adaptogens (see page 93), this herb boosts energy levels, beats exhaustion and reduces the effects of stress on the body. It was used by Russian cosmonauts to increase stamina and studies suggest that it may be helpful in treating jetlag and reducing altitude sickness.

SKULLCAP *Scutellaria laterifolia*
A safe and effective herb that is used to alleviate anxiety and support the nervous system. It calms without sedating, so is particularly useful in helping with stressful situations in which it is important for the mind to remain clear, such as presentations and exams. Skullcap can be helpful for tension headaches and is an excellent addition to a sleep tea as it helps to reduce anxious, circular thoughts.

SLIPPERY ELM *Ulmus fulva* 💚 💧
The dried inner bark of the slippery elm tree is usually sold as a powder. It is incomparable for soothing and healing

the internal surfaces of the digestive system. It is widely used for dyspepsia and any condition in which the mucus membranes are affected, such as IBS, diarrhoea, coughs, urinary tract infections and sore throats.

SPEARMINT *Mentha spicata*
Spearmint is used to cool and settle the stomach, reduce nausea and improve digestion, and in the treatment of IBS and inflammation of the gallbladder. It is also used for sore throats, colds, headaches and pain relief. Its flavour is brighter and less spicy than peppermint, making it a delicious addition to herb teas.

ST JOHN'S WORT *Hypericum perforatum* 💚 ⬦ [particularly antidepressants and oral contraceptives]
Numerous studies suggest that this herb has an important role to play in the treatment of mild to moderate depression. Its effects are not immediate and it takes several weeks of consistent use to start feeling the difference it can make. St John's wort is particularly helpful in Seasonal Affective Disorder (SAD), especially when used alongside light therapy. It can also help in managing mood swings in menopause. Less well-known are its antiviral effects – it is used both internally and externally to treat viral infections such as chickenpox and shingles. If you are on medication, do consult a doctor or herbalist before using St John's wort as the herb has a stimulating effect on the liver, which can reduce the effects of medication.

STAR ANISE *Illicium verum* 💚 💧
A star anise seed makes an attractive and unusual garnish in a herb tea, while its aniseed flavour lends sweetness. It is traditionally used in its native China to treat coughs and colds as well as to reduce gas, increase appetite and even as an aphrodisiac. It has also been used to ease the pain of childbirth.

THYME LEAVES *Thymus vulgaris* 💚
Thyme is highly antimicrobial and an excellent herb to include in gargles for sore throats and mouthwashes for oral infections. It is also an effective expectorant, helping to dislodge and expel mucus in coughs and chest infections.

TULSI *Ocimum sanctum* 💚 💧
Also known as Holy basil, this herb is considered sacred in India where it is widely grown and used. It has a host of benefits, from balancing blood sugar to lowering high blood pressure. It is used to treat coughs and colds and for support during times of stress and anxiety.

TURMERIC *Curcuma longa* 💚 [blood-thinning medication]
Numerous studies have confirmed the anti-inflammatory effects of this bright yellow spice. Try it to reduce pain and inflammation in arthritis and sports injuries as well as more general inflammatory conditions. Turmeric also supports good liver function and has been used to balance levels of cholesterol in the blood. As a powerful antioxidant it may help in the prevention and treatment of cancer.

VERVAIN *Verbena officinalis* 💚
Cooling and a little bitter, vervain is primarily used to treat the nervous system. It helps to reduce stress and relax tense muscles. It is a useful herb to add to a sleep remedy as it is traditionally considered to drive away nightmares and ensure a restful sleep.

VIOLET *Viola odorata*
Intensely fragrant, sweet violet flowers are a spring-time favourite – a small vase full of them can scent an entire room. The flowers are harvested for medicine, but are so tiny that it is mainly the leaves that are used to treat upper respiratory infections and excessive catarrh. Violet is also taken for itchy skin conditions such as eczema and has been used for urinary infections.

WILD YAM ROOT *Dioscorea villosa* [oestrogen-sensitive conditions]
A powerful anti-inflammatory herb with pain-killing properties, wild yam is used to treat all kinds of joint problems, particularly rheumatoid arthritis. It has a particular affinity with internal inflammatory, spasmodic conditions such as period pain, colic and bowel spasms. This herb was the original source of hormone material for the contraceptive pill and may help to balance female hormones.

WILLOW BARK *Salix alba/nigra* [aspirin allergy]
Like meadowsweet, willow bark contains salicylic acid, the anti-inflammatory and pain-killing constituent in aspirin. It is consequently an excellent herb to use in the treatment of inflammation and pain anywhere in the body, and is used in particular to treat arthritis and connective tissue diseases. A high level of tannins in the herb helps to protect the stomach lining, which can be damaged by conventional aspirin.

WOOD BETONY *Stachys betonica*
Wood betony is one of the best herbs to treat headaches and neuralgia (nerve pain), particularly in the face. It is said to have a grounding effect, making it a useful tool for meditation and when experiencing anxiety and stress.

YARROW *Achillea millefolium* 💚
Once known as soldier's wound wort, yarrow is a great styptic (it can stop bleeding when applied to a wound) and, used externally, reduces the effects of bites and stings. By promoting blood flow to the skin, it can help to relieve high blood pressure and promotes sweating, making it useful for treating colds and fevers. It is an antibiotic and kills the bacteria that can cause urinary and other infections.

YELLOW DOCK ROOT *Rumex crispus* 💚
Yellow dock is an effective but relatively gentle laxative, promoting good bowel function for occasional constipation. It is stimulating to the liver and gall bladder and, by helping to promote good excretory function, is widely used to treat skin diseases such as eczema, psoriasis and acne.

Resources

It is important to buy your herbs from a reputable supplier, and also to get advice from a herbalist recognized by his or her professional body before experimenting with herbs. All of the herbs in this book are safe, providing they are not contraindicated for any health condition you may have, or medication you may be taking. If you are in doubt, it is always a good idea to check with a registered herbalist.

UK

National Institute of
Medical Herbalists

The leading professional body representing herbal practitioners in the UK

Clover House
James Court
South Street
Exeter
EX1 1EE
+44 (0) 1392 426022
info@nimh.org.uk
www.nimh.org.uk

SUPPLIERS

G. Baldwin & Co.
171–173 Walworth Road
London
SE17 1RW
+44 (0) 20 7703 5550
www.baldwins.co.uk

Napiers the Herbalists
18 Bristo Place
Edinburgh
EH1 1EZ
+44 (0) 131 263 1860
advice@napiers.net
www.napiers.net

Neal's Yard Remedies
Visit the website for details of local stores

Peacemarsh
Gillingham
Dorset
SP8 4EU
+44 (0) 845 262 3145
nyrdirect@nealsyardremedies.com
www.nealsyardremedies.com

Just Ingredients
PO Box 146
Chepstow
Monmouthshire
NP16 9AH
+44 (0) 1291 635525
sales@justingredients.co.uk
www.justingredients.co.uk

Canada

Canadian Council of Herbalist
Associations (CCHA)

Represents associations of herbal practitioners across Canada

CCHA/CCAH
362 Ste-Catherine
Longueuil
Québec J4H 2C1
www.herbalccha.org

SUPPLIERS

Richters Herbs
357 Highway 47
Goodwood ON L0C 1A0
+1 905 640 6677
www.richters.com

Monteagle Herbs
14 Lake Street, #3
PO Box 258
Killaloe ON K0J 2A0
+1 613 757 0796
peter@monteagleherbs.com
www.monteagleherbs.com

Premier Herbal
109 Dolomite Drive
Toronto ON M3J 2N1
+1 905 761 6266
info@premierherbal.ca
www.premierherbal.ca

USA

American Herbalists Guild

The professional body representing herbalists in the USA

PO Box 3076
Asheville
NC 28802-3076
+1 617 520 4372
office@americanherbalistsguild.com
www.americanherbalistsguild.com

SUPPLIERS

Mountain Rose Herbs
PO Box 50220
Eugene
OR 97405
+1 541 741 7307
support@mountainroseherbs.com
www.mountainroseherbs.com

Pacific Botanicals
4840 Fish Hatchery Road Grants Pass
OR 97527
+1 541 479 7777
www.pacificbotanicals.com

Starwest Botanicals
161 Main Ave
Sacramento
CA 95838
+1 916 638 8100
Toll Free 1 (800) 800 4372
www.starwest-botanicals.com

Bulk Herb Store
38 3rd Avenue East
Lobelville
TN 37097
+1 877 278 4257
info@bulkherbstore.com
www.bulkherbstore.com

Zack Woods Herb Farm
278 Mead Road
Hyde Park
VT 05655
+1 802 888 7278
zackwoodsherbfarm@gmail.com
www.zackwoodsherbs.com

Australia and New Zealand

National Herbalists of Australia
(NHAA)

*The professional body representing
Western herbalists in Australia*

PO Box 696
Ashfield NSW 1800
Australia
+61 (0) 2 9797 2244
nhaa@nhaa.org.au
www.nhaa.org.au

New Zealand Association of Medical
Herbalists (NZAMH)

*The professional organization for
qualified medical herbalists and
naturopaths in New Zealand*

PO Box 12582
Chartwell
Hamilton, 3248
New Zealand
+64 (07) 855 6724
info@nzmah.org.nz
www.nzamh.org.nz

SUPPLIERS

Austral Herbs
PO Box 22
Uralla NSW 2358
Australia
+61 (0) 2 6778 7357
herbs@australherbs.com.au
www.australherbs.com.au

Herb Cottage
491 Gold Coast Springbrook Road
Mudgeeraba 4213
Queensland
Australia
+61 (0) 7 553 032 53

sandra@herbcottage.com.au
www.herbcottage.com.au

Herb Wholesalers
9 Chiswick Place
Forest Lake
Queensland 4078
Australia
+61 (0) 7 3200 1900
sales@herbwholesalers.com
www.herbwholesalers.com

Southern Light Herbs
P.O Box 227
Maldon
Victoria 3463
Australia
+61 (0) 3 5475 2763
info@southernlightherbs.com.au
www.wouthernlightherbs.com.au

New Zealand Botanicals
PO Box 9048
Greerton
Tauranga 3142
New Zealand
+64 (07) 574 4974
www.nzbotanicals.com

Cottage Hill Herb Farm
2 Bridge Road
Birchville
Upper Hutt 5018
New Zealand
+64 (04) 526 4753
donna@cottagehillherbs.co.nz
www.cottagehillherbs.co.nz

Index

Achy Joint Tea 66
agrimony 34, 43, 132
Ah-tea-shoo! 90
albizia 51, 112, 132
All in the Mind 80
Allergy-ease Cordial 126
allspice 118, 132
Almond Milk 123, 127
andrographis 18, 98, 132
angelica root 18, 44, 48, 132
aniseed 31, 40, 74, 132
Aptogenius Tea 93
ashwagandha 93, 104, 130, 132
astragalus 86, 96, 132

bacopa 57, 132
bearberry 29, 132–3
bilberries 25, 133
Bitter & Twisted 48
black cohosh 82, 133
black horehound 42, 133
black peppercorns 133
blackberry leaf 34, 133
Bladder Bliss 29
Blood Sugar Balancer 67
blood sugar levels 7, 51, 67
blue flag root 26, 133
Bon Courage! 75
boneset 98, 133
Boost & Revitalize 8, 53–67
borage 75, 111, 133
buchu 29, 133
burdock 26, 133
buying dried herbs 11–12

calendula 15, 26, 32, 108, 133
Californian poppy 74, 133
caraway seeds 44, 133
cardamom 44, 50, 104, 118, 121, 133
catmint leaves 72, 96, 133
cayenne pepper 133
celery seeds 31, 66, 134
Chai Honey 118
chamomile 15, 18, 19, 40, 44, 47, 72, 80, 96, 107, 108, 134
chaste tree berries 82, 134

chicory 54, 134
chocolate 121
cinnamon 19, 31, 35, 44, 67, 89, 99, 115, 118, 121, 123, 134
Clean Seeds Tea 31
cleavers 26, 32, 134
cloves 18, 39, 118, 134
Commuter Protection 89
Conval-essence 96
Cool It! 63
coriander seeds 39, 40, 48, 115, 134
corn silk 29, 134
couch grass 18, 29, 134
cramp bark 34, 40, 76, 134

damiana 58, 60, 61, 104, 106, 134
dandelion 15, 23, 28, 32, 54, 76, 134
decoctions 18
devil's claw 66, 134
Digesti-tea 47
dill seeds 44, 134
DIY tea blends 18–19
drying herbs for tea 15–16

echinacea 18, 89, 90, 98, 99, 120, 127, 134
elderberries 25, 86, 89, 99, 115, 120, 127, 135
elderflowers 63, 90, 98, 108, 126, 135
elecampane 48, 95, 135
equipment 11, 19
eyebright 90, 126, 135

fennel seed 31, 44, 50, 54, 65, 104, 108, 126, 135
fenugreek 31, 65, 135
feverfew 80, 135
figwort 26, 135
Flower Garden Tea 124
Fresh Herb Sorbet 129
Fruity Antioxidant Burst 25
Fussy, Feverish Kids' Tea 96

garlic 120
Get Up and Go Tea 60
gifts 19

ginger 7, 12, 18, 135
  Aptogenius Tea 93
  Chai Honey 118
  Clean Seeds Tea 31
  In the Mood 106
  Memory Boost Tea 57
  Monthly Magic 76
  Morning Cleanse 23
  No More Nausea 42
  Nourishing Rooibos Chai 39
  Study-aid Tea 61
  Tea for a Head Cold 99
  Tummy Warmer Tea 44
  Vital Force Tea 104
  Winter Blues Tea 113
  Winter Warmer 90
gingko leaf 57, 61, 135
goats' rue 67, 135
Golden Milk 123
goldenrod 29, 90, 135
gotu kola 57, 135
grinding herbs 16–18
Gut Reaction 51
Gut Soother 47

Happy Tea 103
hawthorn 25, 34, 92, 112, 115, 135
Healthy Honey 120
heartsease 112, 135
hibiscus flowers 25, 104, 111, 136
Holiday Celebration Tea 115
holy basil see tulsi (holy basil)
honey 12, 19, 98, 118, 120
hop flowers 72, 136
horsetail 32, 136
Hot Spiced Cocoa 121
hyssop 95, 129, 136

Immune-boosting Smoothie 127
Immuni-tea 86
In the Mood 106
Is it Warm in Here? 83

Jamaican dogwood 76, 136
jasmine flowers 74, 106, 136

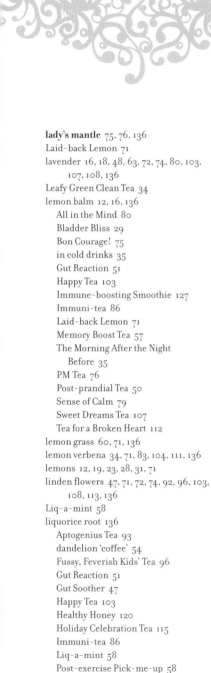

lady's mantle 75, 76, 136
Laid-back Lemon 71
lavender 16, 18, 48, 63, 72, 74, 80, 103,
   107, 108, 136
Leafy Green Clean Tea 34
lemon balm 12, 16, 136
   All in the Mind 80
   Bladder Bliss 29
   Bon Courage! 75
   in cold drinks 35
   Gut Reaction 51
   Happy Tea 103
   Immune-boosting Smoothie 127
   Immuni-tea 86
   Laid-back Lemon 71
   Memory Boost Tea 57
   The Morning After the Night
     Before 35
   PM Tea 76
   Post-prandial Tea 50
   Sense of Calm 79
   Sweet Dreams Tea 107
   Tea for a Broken Heart 112
lemon grass 60, 71, 136
lemon verbena 34, 71, 83, 104, 111, 136
lemons 12, 19, 23, 28, 31, 71
linden flowers 47, 71, 72, 74, 92, 96, 103,
   108, 113, 136
Liq-a-mint 58
liquorice root 136
   Aptogenius Tea 93
   dandelion 'coffee' 54
   Fussy, Feverish Kids' Tea 96
   Gut Reaction 51
   Gut Soother 47
   Happy Tea 103
   Healthy Honey 120
   Holiday Celebration Tea 115
   Immuni-tea 86
   Liq-a-mint 58
   Post-exercise Pick-me-up 58
   Post-prandial Tea 50
   Serenitea 108
   Super-soothing Cough Tea 95
   Winter Warmer 90
Lymph-buster Tea 32

marshmallow 18, 29, 35, 47, 115, 136
meadowsweet 47, 51, 58, 66, 96, 136–7
Meditation Tea 108
Memory Boost Tea 57
milk thistle 28, 35, 137
mint 12, 16, 18, 34
   see also peppermint; spearmint
Monthly Magic 76
The Morning After the Night Before 35
Morning Cleanse 23
motherwort 83, 92, 137
Move It! 40
mugwort 48, 74, 75, 108, 137

Nervous Tummy Tea 43
nettle leaf 26, 34, 35, 65, 76, 90, 96, 126, 137
No More Nausea 42
Nourishing Rooibos Chai 39

oat seeds 79, 137
oregano 34, 137
Oregon grape root 28, 48, 137

parsley 23, 137
passionflower 72, 79, 137
Peace & Calm 8, 69–83
peppermint 42, 47, 50, 58, 60, 65, 90, 96,
   99, 127, 137
plantain 47, 51, 126, 137
Post-exercise Pick-me-up 58
Post-prandial Tea 50

raspberry leaf 34, 65, 137–8
red clover 26, 32, 74, 83, 138
rhodiola 93, 113, 138
rhubarb root 40, 138
rooibos 39, 113, 138
rose geranium leaves 138
rose petals 79, 82, 103, 104, 106, 108, 111,
   112, 138
rosehips 66, 89, 115, 138
rosemary 18, 48, 57, 61, 80, 104, 108,
   113, 138

sage 12, 63, 82, 83, 89, 95, 120, 138
St John's wort 7, 82, 96, 98, 113, 139

sarsaparilla 26, 60, 138
schisandra berries 28, 96, 138
Sense of Calm 79
Serenitea 108
shatavari root 82, 138
Siberian ginseng 35, 60, 67, 104,
   106, 138
Skin Fix 26
skullcap 34, 61, 71, 75, 79, 138
slippery elm 47, 138–9
spearmint 34, 58, 63, 80, 90, 111, 139
star anise 44, 139
storing dried herbs 12
Stress Headache Tea 80
Study-aid Tea 61
Summer Lovin' 111
Super-soothing Cough Tea 95
Sweet Dreams Tea 107

Tea for a Broken Heart 112
Tea for a Head Cold 99
tea balls/infusers 11, 19
teapots 11, 19
thyme 12, 18, 86, 95, 120, 139
Time of Your Life Tea 82
TLC (Tea for Liver Care) 28
tulsi (holy basil) 51, 57, 67, 79, 104,
   108, 139
Tummy Warmer Tea 44
turmeric 66, 123, 139

vervain 34, 107, 108, 139
violet 63, 139
Vital Force Tea 104

water 18
When it's Flu Tea 98
wild yam root 51, 58, 139
wildcrafting 12–15
willow bark 66, 139
Winter Blues Tea 113
Winter Warmer 90
wood betony 80, 107, 112, 139

yarrow 16, 92, 99, 126, 139
yellow dock root 40, 139

Acknowledgements

PAULA

Thanks to Karen Sullivan and Gill Paul for making this happen. I am so grateful to everyone who has entrusted the herbs and me with their health over the years, and who have taught me so much. Love to all who made Lemon Balm such an amazing experience – too many to list, but especially Jenny Andrews, Daniel Baumann and Shirley Zerf, who were there all the way. Thank you to my Santa Cruz folk: Karen, Lisa, Darren, Kea and Matt, who helped make this a home, and Dad, Marie, Karen, Rob, Wendy, David, Tes, Eleanor, Dena and Zaz in the UK, who make sure I have a home there, too. In fond memory of Mum and Nanny, who passed on their love of plants and didn't mind my early herbal experiments cluttering their kitchens. Most of all, eternal thanks to the love of my life, Michael, for sharing over 20 years of life, love and harebrained schemes, and to the light of my life, Nate, for being our boy.

KAREN

I'd like to thank Paula Grainger, Leanne Bryan and Salima Hirani for being such professionals – inspiring and a joy to work with. Thanks also to my very patient family, Max, Cole, Luke and Marcus, and to my cousin Erica Manger, who shares my love of natural health.

Commissioning Editor Leanne Bryan
Designers Jaz Bahra and Isabel de Cordova
Photographer Mowie Kay
Food Stylist Maud Eden
Prop Stylist Jessica Georgiades
Copy Editor Salima Hirani
Production Controller Allison Gonsalves

An Hachette UK Company
www.hachette.co.uk

First published in Great Britain in 2016 by Hamlyn, a division of Octopus Publishing Group Ltd, Carmelite House, 50 Victoria Embankment, London EC4Y 0DZ
www.octopusbooks.co.uk

Copyright © Octopus Publishing Group Ltd 2016

ISBN 978-0-600-63283-2

A CIP catalogue record for this book is available from the British Library.

Printed and bound in China.

10 9 8 7 6 5 4 3 2 1

This book is designed to educate and entertain and the authors do not claim that the recipes treat medical conditions. Before self-medicating with herbs, it is recommended that readers consult a medical professional – particularly if they are pregnant or nursing, have an existing medical condition or are taking prescribed medication. Any application of the ideas and information contained in this book is at the reader's sole discretion and risk.